The complete book of

Sports Cars

Picture Credits:

Neill Bruce Motoring Photolibrary
28-29, 88-89, 164, 184-185, 275, 276-277, 279, 280-281, 282-283, 284-285

Jaguar Cars
240-241, 242-243, 244-245, 277

McLaren Cars Ltd.
15, 274

Maserati
208-209

Andrew Morland
165

Peter Roberts Collection
286-287, 288

All other illustrations: CLB International

This edition first published in 2002 by Crestline, an imprint of MBI Publishing Company, Galtier Plaza, Suite 200, 380 Jackson Street, St. Paul, MN 55101-3885 USA

© Salamander Books Ltd., 2002

A member of **Chrysalis** Books plc

MBI Publishing Company books are also available at discounts in bulk quantity for industrial or sales-promotional use. For details write to Special Sales Manager at Motorbooks International Wholesalers & Distributors, Galtier Plaza, Suite 200, 380 Jackson Street, St. Paul, MN 55101-3885 USA.

Library of Congress Cataloging-in-Publication Data Available

ISBN 0-7603-1455-1

Printed in China

The complete book of

Sports Cars

Bill Reynolds

Updated and revised by Mirco De Cet

CRESTLINE

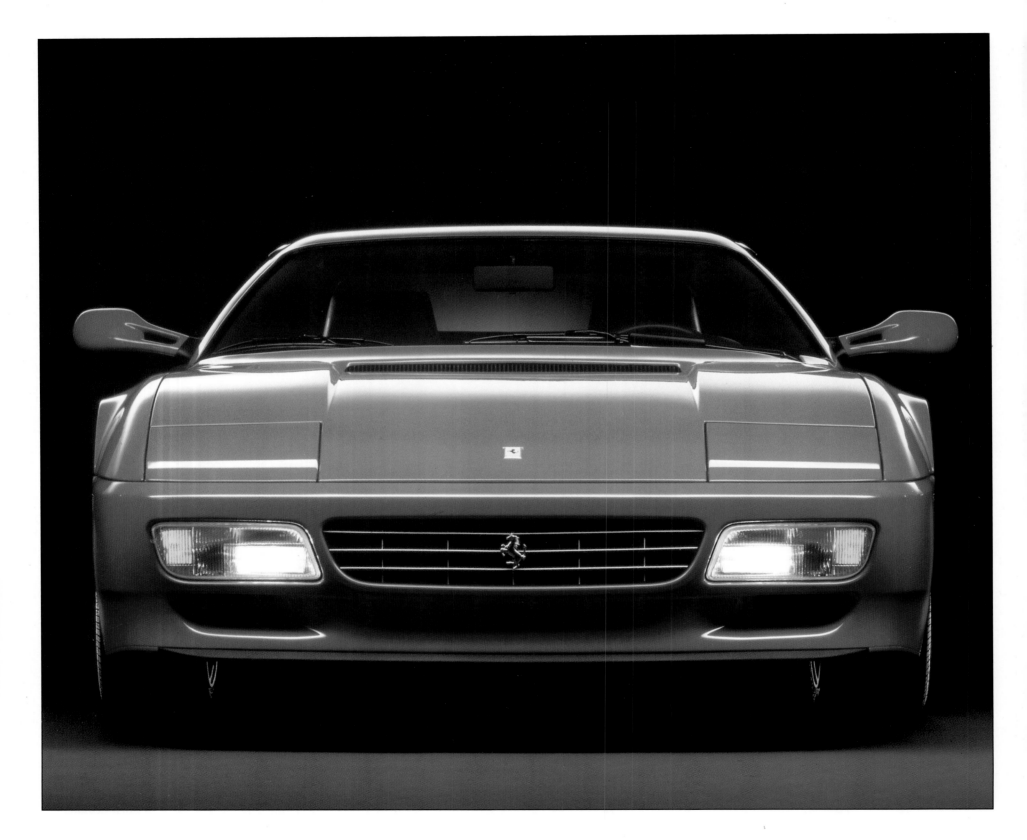

CONTENTS

Left: the 1992 Ferrari 512 TR

INTRODUCTION

Sports cars are easier to recognize than to define. To some, you must be able to race them. To others, light weight is everything. To yet others, an open top is an essential prerequisite. The number of seats can also be a defining factor: any more than two (or perhaps three, with a nod to Matra and McLaren), and many would say that it isn't a sports car.

In these pages, I have adopted a simple, relaxed, and ultimately rather personal definition. A sports car must have above average performance for its time, but it need not be a racer. It must also capture the spirit of the age, and the imagination of the automobile-buying public, either at the time or later. A great sports car is a blend of 'show' and 'go'.

Much as it may offend the purists, this question of image is at least as important as performance. Some manufacturers have exploited this mercilessly: a number of truly appalling cars have been sold on the back of a sporting image. The sad truth, too, is that most of the people who can actually afford to buy new sports cars are all too willing to make compromises on sheer performance, in return for comfort, quietness, ease of driving and reliability.

PERFORMANCE FIGURES

It is instructive to see how cars have changed over the years. The earliest models of the Porsche 356, for example, were advertised as having a top speed of 87 mph (140 km/h). Weight was around 1850-1900 lb. With only 40 bhp, this gave a power-to-weight ratio of 47 bhp/tonne.

When the Porsche 911 was introduced in 1964, the 1991cc engine delivered 130 bhp, but weight had gone up to 2367 lb so the power-to-weight ratio was 120 bhp/tonne. Top speed was about 130 mph (210 km/h).

In 1996, you could buy a production Porsche 911 Turbo, off the shelf, not a competition model, with 408 bhp

from 3600cc: 113 bhp/litre. It weighed 3300 lb: 272 bhp/tonne. It could top 180 mph (290 km/h).

Of course, power-to-weight ratios do not tell the whole story. Modern tyres offer better grip than old ones, and are wider too, so today's cars go round corners better, are less prone to wheelspin, and stop better. Disc brakes are far more efficient than drums, and lighter. Drag coefficients have not so much dropped as plummeted, translating into better top-end performance and better fuel economy. Fuel injection and electronic engine management have transformed efficiency. Better fuels mean that the ritual of the 'decoke', or cylinder head decarbonization, is no longer regularly performed to keep engines in top condition. Modern lubricants sap less power and allow tighter tolerances.

RAW SPEED AND ACCELERATION

Once 100 mph had become a speed to which most people could, at least in theory, aspire, the next goal was either 120 mph (194 km/h) or 200 km/h (124 mph). This sort of speed is, however, a very different kettle of fish. Unlike 100 mph, it is rarely achievable on ordinary roads, so you need autobahns or their equivalents.

Regardless of the legal limit, the vast majority of people on autobahns tend to travel at around 60 to 85 mph, or maybe 100 to 135 km/h. At 200 km/h, the speed differential starts to make a real difference. You are going almost three times as fast as the slowest driver; twice as fast as the average slow driver; and almost fifty per cent faster than the average fast driver.

In practical terms, therefore, the maximum speeds of modern sports cars are substantially irrelevant. Anything much over 150 mph or 250 km/h is principally of academic interest. Yes, you may be able to test your car's maximum speed, once or twice, at five in the morning on a summer's day; but you are never going to be able to use it on a regular basis. For credibility's sake, you need a comfortable margin over 125 mph (200 km/h), but you are not going to use it very often.

What is more important than top speed in practical terms is acceleration, and there is a cultural difference here. Americans tend to prize acceleration from a standing start, but care little for nimbleness, while Europeans are often more interested in acceleration from high speeds when coupled with a readiness to respond to the steering wheel.

This is a more fundamental difference than it might seem. It affects not only the approach to power-to-weight ratios, but also torque distribution and even the gearbox layout of a 5-speed. An American wants a broad torque spread, with plenty of bottom end, while a European may be more content with an engine that has to be kept 'on the cam.' Likewise, a European will want first in the dog-leg, allowing ready swapping at high speed between fourth and fifth, which are in a single plane; while an American will want fifth in the dog-leg, where it functions as a cruising gear, while retaining first and second in a single plane to allow the fastest possible gear-changes from a standing start.

'SHOW' AND 'GO'

Regardless of performance, there is no doubt that some sports cars are inherently better looking than others — but even here, we run into many different criteria. There are the classicists, and the exoticists, and the functionalists, and the brutalists, all with their different ideas about what a sports car should look like. For that matter, some cars are immeasurably improved by having their tops sawn off. The Jaguar XJS is a handsome grand tourer in hard-top guise, but as a drop-head it seems far more of a sports car. And while your head may tell you that Ferrari's Berlinetta hard-tops may be faster, lighter and stronger, your heart tells you that the Spyder soft-tops are the real sports cars, not the coupés.

Ultimately, this allows some cars to claim the 'sports' label even when it is patently unjustified in performance terms, but there are times when the heart must take precedence over the head — or even the right foot, which is why the selection of cars in this book (or any book like it) is inevitably personal, disputable, and indeed on occasion downright quixotic. This book may be even more so than usual, as I have chosen to concentrate on five great marques that embody different attitudes towards sports cars. The majority of the pictures in the pages that follow are therefore of Ferraris, Jaguars, Porsches, Corvettes and Mustangs, though wherever necessary I have introduced other significant vehicles.

To simplify matters still further, I have broken the half–century covered (actually, it's a little more) into five periods of somewhat uneven length. These are first, the immediate post-war period from 1945 to 1955; second, 1956 to 1962, the period of enormous increase in power; third, the flowering of many different design philosophies from 1963 to 1973; fourth, the rather dull time from 1974 to 1982, when only a few cars kept the faith and a lot of sports cars looked more like appliances; and fifth, the renaissance of the sports car since about 1983.

POST-WAR SPORTS CARS – 1945-1955

After World War II, Ferrari was the first into the fray, as a brand-new company with a brand-new 1500cc V12, the Tipo 125 in 1946. This never had as much power as Enzo Ferrari wanted, so he kept making it bigger: first the Tipo 166 (two litre, 1948), then Tipo 195 (2.3 litre, 1949), then Tipo 212 (2.5 litre, 1949), then Tipo 340 (4 litre, the new Lampredi-designed engine in 1952), then Tipo 375 (4.5 litre, 1953). Not until 1954 was this trend reversed with the 3-litre 250 GT Europa. All through the period, Ferrari made V12s, usually very lightly built and very much in the tradition of sports-racers.

In 1948, though, Jaguar set the big cat among the pigeons with a very different style of motor-car: very fast, stunningly good looking, and astonishingly affordable. So successful was it that it effectively redefined the genre and made the T-series MG and the Morgan look like the pre-war vehicles they in essence were. The Triumph TR2 and the MGA were both direct consequences of the XK120, which bridged the gap between 'supercars' and affordable sports cars in a way that is hardly imaginable today. In 1954, the XK140 was an altogether plumper Jaguar, but it was still very, very fast.

Meanwhile, Porsche had also crept onto the scene. They made about four cars in 1948, a couple of dozen the next year, and about 400 in 1950. By 1953, annual production was still under 2,000. By contrast, over 12,000 XK120s were made from 1949 to 1954.

Admittedly, Porsche started winning races from day one, but they were very much 'class' wins for small, low-powered sports cars: the Jaguar, with 160 bhp to propel 2920 lb, had 120 bhp/tonne where the Porsche had 40. For comparison, a Ferrari 166 Inter of 1951 had 110 bhp in base form and weighed 2000 lb: about 120 bhp/tonne again, the same as the Jaguar.

Across the pond, Briggs Cunningham made a valiant attempt to introduce an American sports car, but it was never quite competitive and he quit the unequal struggle after five years, during which he lost a reputed $50,000 a year. With a Chrysler Hemi engine and Michelotti/Vignale bodywork, it was something of a 'bitsa' in the tradition of the Austin-Healey 100/4 (1954). Studebaker's Commander State Regal Hardtop (1953) had an appalling name for a beautiful sports coupe powered by a 289 cid V8, and unexpectedly, Kaiser's swan-song was the Darrin (1954), a 'glass bodied 100 mph vehicle which arguably sprang from the same inspiration as the incomparably better looking Corvette.

The '53 Corvette looked gorgeous, but few were made and performance was modest: the original 3442cc straight six delivered a miserable 150 bhp SAE. The contemporary TR2 offered similar acceleration, and more top end if properly prepped, from 1991cc. Not until the arrival of the 265 cid (4343cc) V8 for '55 could the Corvette be taken seriously. Even then, of the 700 '55 models sold, more had the straight six than the V8. For comparison, Ford sold 16,000 Thunderbirds.

The T-Bird illustrated only too well the difference between the American and European markets. Yes, it was pretty, and yes, the 4.8 litre Mercury V8 would propel it to around 115 mph (185 km/h) — in a straight line. But heaven help you if you wanted to turn corners!

Compare that with the Lotus 6 of 1952 to 1956, later to metamorphose into the Lotus Seven, and still with us today as the Caterham Seven. Essentially a four-wheeled motorcycle, everything was sacrificed on the altar of handling, and weight was kept to a minimum to make the most of small, light, and often modestly powered engines.

TURNING UP THE WICK – 1956-1962

In 1956, the Porsche 356A could be had with the 1500GS engine delivering well over 100 bhp (DIN): fifty per cent more than the maximum available in the previous year. The Corvette offered a maximum of 240 bhp (SAE), after about 195 bhp (SAE) the previous year: better than a 20 per cent increase. Jaguar had tuned the XK engine to give 250 bhp the previous year, though 210 bhp was normal for the sports version of the XK140; 50 bhp more than the XK120 as originally introduced. Ferrari claimed 400 bhp from the four-litre Lampredi-block V12, between 60 and 100 bhp more than the previous year's most powerful sports-car engines, while the Corvette went from 290 bhp in 1958 to 315 bhp in 1960 to a maximum of 360 bhp from the 327 cid engine in 1961 (when the least powerful model was 250 bhp).

Power was, however, often allied to glory. The most noteworthy new car in the period, as in the previous period, arguably came from Jaguar. In 1962 their E-type (sometimes called the XK-E) replaced the XK150, itself a 1957 replacement for the XK140. No less than 400 lb lighter than the XK150, with 265 bhp to speed its 2464 lb to 150 mph (242 km/h), it returned Jaguar to the supercar league. Of course it was expensive, but at $5595 in the important US market, it was around half the price of a Ferrari 250GT; had ten per cent more power (the road Ferrari claimed 240 bhp, or 280 bhp for the racer); weighed much the same; and had about the same top speed.

Hand in hand with increasing power and improving handling (at least from some manufacturers) came increasing luxury and sophistication. Not from all models, to be sure: Lotus kept the faith with the Seven, and although the fibreglass Elite (1957) with its Coventry Climax engine delivering 71 to 95 bhp was more car-like, racing tricks like fixed side windows meant you still had to prize 'go' over 'show' to drive one. But Aston Martin, for all their racing heritage, offered automatic transmission as an option on their DB 2/4 MkIII (1958). Another option was 195 bhp instead of 180 bhp; well over 150 bhp/tonne. But then, the DB4 of the same year had 240 bhp, well over 180 bhp/tonne.

Despite general improvements on all sides, there were still some 'parts bin' cars, or 'straight line specials'. Ford, for example, offered a truly terrifying supercharged version of the T-Bird in 1957, with 325 bhp from 5.1 litres. It could hit 60 mph in 7 seconds, and go on to 125 mph (200 km/h) — still with handling like a pig on roller-skates. As it turned out, 1957 was the last year for the 'classic' T-birds, but over 53,000 were made and sold.

MID-ENGINES AND MORE – 1963-1973

Ferrari's 250 LM V12 of 1963 effectively started the fashion for mid-mounted engines for sports cars, as well as for racers. Admittedly, it was essentially a competition car, but the Dino of 1965 was very much a road car. At that time, of course, it was not officially a Ferrari, being named after Enzo's beloved son. The 1963 model year also saw the Sting Ray, a rather different departure for the Corvette. Unlike its traditional, 'hairy chested' forebears, the Sting Ray was a fixed head coupé of much more purposeful mien.

A year later, in 1964, Porsche started to sell the 6-cylinder 911: it differed far more than the 356 from the Volkswagen which sired the marque. In April of the same year, the first Mustang came out as a '1964-½'. All four of these cars, superficially very different, marked a sea-change in sports car design. The first generation after World War II had been sports/racers. The second generation had seen the gap between sports and racing cars widening. This, the third generation, marked a departure from the way that things had been done before: the manufacturers were clearly re-thinking what a sports car should be, and how they could best produce one.

Admittedly, the break was not (except in the case of Porsche) absolutely abrupt or decisive. Ferrari continued to sell a wild range of car layouts and types with V6 and V12 engines, even introducing a V8 in 1973. The Sting Ray still had some features which were more 'show' than 'go', such as the lethal split rear window with its abysmal visibility, and it did not acquire four-wheel discs as standard until 1965. Power continued to climb: the '66 Corvette had at least 425 bhp from a 427 cid (7 litre) engine, and the L88 engine (a 1967 Corvette option) delivered 560 bhp on 103 octane fuel. The new-look 1968 Corvettes, on the other hand, had beautiful styling but absolutely nothing else going for them: this was the car which *Car and Driver* refused to road test, because it was so badly built. Somewhat depressingly, the beastly thing sold in huge numbers.

Throughout the period, Porsche continued to improve the 911, which had initially frightened more than a few people with its light nose and tail-happy demeanour: one of the first modifications involved bolting lead weights inside the ends of the front bumper to keep the nose down. In 1963, the flat six delivered 130 bhp DIN, 148 bhp SAE; in 1969 the most powerful 911S option was up to 180 bhp SAE; and by 1973, it was 181 bhp SAE net, which is around 200 bhp under the old SAE system.

Actually, Porsche also introduced a mid-engined car of their own in 1970, the 914. In a sense, it marked a return to their roots as builders of fast, light cars, and it also marked a closer liaison with Volkswagen (who were supposed to sell a down-rated version as a Volkswagen sports car), but unfortunately it was startlingly ugly. It could have been a contender — the six-cylinder racing version was very quick — but it never caught the public imagination, and most Porsche fans seem happy to forget both the 914/4 flat four and the 914/6 flat six.

Jaguar's E-type put on weight steadily, faster than the straight six could handle; but in 1971, a new 5.3 litre V12 engine appeared with 272 bhp DIN, 250 bhp SAE net. Top speed was still below the magic 150 mph which had been (just) achievable with the earliest E-types, but equally, it was well over 130 mph (210 km/h), and it was achieved with great ease and style.

The Mustang, meanwhile, reached its apotheosis with the 1965 Cobra (306 bhp in road form, or 350 bhp for the racer — and the race car could be driven on the road). Unfortunately, it then began a slow but steady decline. In 1966 the limited-slip diff and the Koni shocks were made an option; the 'sidewinder' exhausts disappeared; the suspension was downrated; and a Paxton supercharger was made an option, emphasizing the 'straight-line special' mentality of FoMoCo. The 1967 GT500 Cobra was offered with the 427 cid engine and at least 425 bhp, and the 1968 Boss 302 and Boss 429 were very impressive motor cars; but they had passed their peak.

In a sense, though, this was a 'golden age'. Quite apart from the five marques that form the core of our story, established manufacturers such as Alfa Romeo, MG, Triumph, Morgan and Austin Healey continued to make believably priced sports cars; Aston Martin, Ferrari, Maserati and (after 1964) Lamborghini supplied the top end of the market; the AC Cobra delivered spectacularly hairy-chested power, with its big Ford engine in a (relatively) light chassis; Jensen introduced both sporting four-wheel drive and anti-lock braking on the FF (1967); and names like Matra and Marcos first came to the attention of would-be sports car buyers.

HEADS DOWN FOR THE FUEL CRISIS – 1974-1982

Three factors conspired against sports cars in the early 1970s. One was the 'gas crisis' of 1973, which should not have been as unexpected as it was. The second was a widespread belief within the motor industry that American safety legislation would effectively outlaw convertibles. The third, which actually started in the late 1960s, was the decline of the British motor industry.

Although the Italians were always important at the top, the British remained a very significant force in sporting motoring, as they do to this day — just look where most of the world's Formula One cars are built. But with fewer and fewer manufacturers and worse and worse management, there was less and less scope for new talent. Greyness bid fair to destroy the sports car.

Across the pond, Ford fairly leapt off the band-wagon. The 'muscle' Mustangs of the late 1960s and early 1970s had become hypertrophied in any case, so in 1974 the gutless Mustang II was rolled out with a base 2.3-litre four (72 bhp/tonne) and a 2.8-litre V6 (85 bhp/tonne). In either form it could top 100 mph, and in its favour it was a startling 1000 lb or more lighter than the car it replaced; but it wasn't a sports car. Even the return of the 302 cid (5 litre) engine in 1972 meant only 140 bhp overall, 94 bhp/tonne, and for 1980 it was reduced to 4.2 litres and 119 bhp. The turbocharged 2.3-litre four offered 132 bhp: rough, but more power than the V8 and lighter to boot. It was not until 1982 that the power climbed again, to 157 bhp with a return to the 5-litre engine.

Jaguar was wrong-footed, at least twice over. To replace the increasingly porcine E-type, they introduced the XJ-S in 1976. Unfortunately, it was not a ground-breaking sports car in the tradition of the XK120 and the E-type. Rather, it was a grand tourer. It was an extremely fine grand tourer, with plenty of room, and it was very fast: 150 mph was genuinely achievable as often as not, quite unlike the late E-types. But it wasn't the car people wanted or expected; it wasn't a drop-head; and it was alarmingly thirsty.

Nor were Corvettes much more interesting. The 'Coke bottle' body was now slightly more sorted than it had been, but emission controls on the one hand and the fuel crisis on the other meant that performance suffered. The '74 Corvette could accelerate from 0 to 60 mph in 7.5 seconds and hit 125 mph, but this was not exactly cutting edge: 5 mph slower than a Porsche 911, 10 to 15 mph slower than the increasingly outmoded E-type, and a staggering 30 mph slower than a Ferrari 365 GT4 BB. Admittedly, the Ferrari was close to three times the price, but it seemed than an enormous and ever-widening gulf separated 'affordable' sports cars from supercars: 1976 was the year the Corvette broke the $10,000 barrier, which was the same year the XJS was introduced at $19,000 and a Ferrari 308 GTB cost $28,580.

The fuel crisis may have affected Ferrari's sales, but it did not have much influence on the type of cars they sold. The Daytona, introduced in 1968, survived until 1974, but the range of new introductions continued to be dazzling every year. For 1974 there was the Tipo 365 GT4 BB flat twelve; in 1975, the Type 308 GTB V-8; in 1976, the 400i V12 'family' Ferrari and the 512 BB flat-twelve, with 344 bhp DIN and a top speed of around 188 mph, just over 300 km/h (at $85,000); in 1980, the Mondial V8; and all the time, more power from existing engines. More valves, fuel injection instead of carburetters, more and more of everything — including, unfortunately, weight on some models. Who would have dreamed of air conditioning, central locking, remote mirrors and a power antenna on a Ferrari? Yet all were standard on the Mondial, and a power sun roof was an option.

The other top-end cars also flourished. Lamborghini's Countach entered production in 1974: over 170 mph (275 km/h) from a 375 bhp, 4-litre V12 in a car weighing around 3600 lb. Maserati's Khamsin was styled by the same person, Marcello Gandini; its 5-litre V8 delivered a mere 320 bhp and the car weighed around 3800 lb, for 185 bhp/tonne instead of the Lamborghini's 230. But it could still top 150 mph with the manual gearbox (auto was an option).

At the bottom end of the market, the news was terrible. Austin-Healey had already disappeared in the 1960s. MG's offerings were hopelessly outdated, and further spoiled by clumsy adaptations to American 'safety' regulations. Triumph's TR7 was ugly, unreliable and slow, and while the same company's Stag was undoubtedly pretty, it was not particularly fast and the engine was notoriously finicky: instead of the obvious choice – the Rover V8 – it had a unique V8 of its own with less power, less reliability and no economies of scale. The Spitfire 1500 was as primitive as an MG — and again slow, especially in American guise where the engine was downrated to 57 bhp because of emission requirements while the weight was boosted with crash bumpers.

Meanwhile, Porsche pursued its own sweet course, getting more and more power out of the 911 and

progressively eradicating its handling defects. The flat six grew to 2687cc in 1974, and while base power was 143 bhp SAE net, the 911S had 167 bhp SAE net in 1975 and the Turbo had 234 bhp SAE net.

Unexpectedly, Porsche also introduced a front engine, rear drive, water-cooled four-cylinder car in 1977, the 924: thus was heresy piled upon heresy. The following year saw a V8 version of the same car, the 928, which was supposed to be a replacement for the 911 — which in the event outlived it. If they had been badged as anything other than Porsches, they would have been greeted with glad cries; but as it was, they did well enough without ever capturing the magic of the 911. Besides, 1978 also saw a 3.3-litre intercooled version of the Turbo with 253 bhp SAE net and a top speed of about 156 mph (over 250 km/h). Next to that, the 928 looked pretty tame with 219 bhp and 133 mph.

RESURGENCE – 1983 ONWARDS

Just as they had led the flight from the sporting image in 1974, Ford led the return in 1983: the Mustang now had 175 bhp from the old V8, or 145 bhp from the turbo, and at long last, the convertible returned.

Sales did not immediately rise, but Ford persevered and in 1984 introduced what was arguably the most sporting Mustang ever, the SVO Turbo four with 175 bhp and all kinds of genuine go-faster goodies, such as Koni shocks at the front, twin shocks each side at the back, bucket seats, 7-inch rubber on 16-inch wheels, and functional aerodynamics including cooling scoops. Unfortunately, it was not really a car for the American market, as it was over 50 per cent more expensive than the 5-litre V8, and its undoubted superiority on the corners had to be set against the fact that the V8 was quicker over the standing quarter. Sales remained poor, at least by Ford's standards, with under 150,000 cars built in 1984.

And that was pretty much where matters stalled. The SVO went up to 205 bhp before it was killed in 1987, while the V8 went up to 225 bhp SAE net, probably close to 275 bhp SAE gross. In 1988 they sold 200,000 of these competent but rather primitive cars, and almost a decade later the so-called Cobra version had a rather cleverer, new V8 but otherwise had not changed very much. Even so, for a few years they had pointed the way...

The Corvette likewise improved greatly in the early-to-mid 1980s. The 1984 model had a completely new chassis, half way to a spaceframe. Weight fell to 3200 lb, and the drag coefficient (Cd) was lowered to 0.35, so even the anachronistic cast iron 350 cid (5.7 litre) V8, with its modest 205 bhp SAE net, could get the car up to 140 mph (226 km/h).

Alas, sales were dire. Once again, the people who could afford such cars showed that they did not want them, while those who wanted them continued to be unable to afford them. A 1986 Corvette cost more than $27,000 – too cheap to be exclusive and too expensive to be affordable.

The 1992 ZR-1 was reassuringly expensive, at $60,000, but equally, it was getting into supercar realms. With 380 bhp from an all-alloy Lotus-designed V8, top speed was around 180 mph — about 10 km/h short of the magic 300 km/h — and this was an astonishingly modest price for what it was. What was really depressing was that even this didn't sell. It was axed less than five years after its introduction, leaving the Corvette in much the same market niche as a Morgan: fast, fun, but stuck in a time warp.

Meanwhile, though, the supercar was becoming a matter of more and more interest among European manufacturers, and Porsche, Jaguar and Ferrari all tried their hand. So did Lamborghini, McLaren, Bugatti and a handful of lesser-known names.

A supercar ought to exceed at least 300 km/h (186 mph) and ideally should top 200 mph (323 km/h), though as little as 155 mph (250 km/h) may be acceptable if it requires a rev limiter to keep it down to that speed. As mentioned above, these top speeds are irrelevant in the sense that they will rarely if ever be reached by the vast majority of owners, but they should make the car easier to drive at more modest speeds because the car is so far inside its 'performance envelope.'

Ferrari, of course, showed the way — though they did not always make the fastest cars. The Testarossa (1984) was a development of the earlier flat 12 supercars, with 380 bhp to propel it to 175-180 mph (280-290 km/h), but the F40 was the defining supercar of 1987: 471 bhp from a twin-turbo V8, 1100 kg (claimed — 2420 lb), and a top speed (again claimed) of 201 mph (325 km/h).

Then, not content with that, they brought out the F50 with a conventionally aspirated race-bred 4.7-litre V12 delivering 513 bhp. Only a tad faster than the F40 at the top end (202 mph instead of 201), it was nevertheless said to be three seconds a lap faster around the Fiorano test track, simply because it is more drivable.

If you want a bit more comfort, then there are always such delights as the 456, touted as the last of the front-engined V12s when it appeared in 1992 but then superseded in 1996 by the 550 Maranello, front engined (V12, of course), rear drive, and with 484 bhp to move even a portly 3640 lb at a claimed 199 mph (321 km/h). Then there is the 355, with a mere 184 mph (297 km/h) top end, but only a quarter of the price of the F50 at £83,000 or so at its 1994 launch.

The trouble was, several people thought they could go faster than Ferrari. At least two of them did: Jaguar, with the XJ220 (213 mph tested, up to 220 mph claimed) and McLaren with the F1 (well in excess of 210 mph, probably over 220 mph). And Lamborghini's Diablo was tested (by *Autocar*) to 202 mph, though it is unclear whether this was based only on a speedometer reading rather than on hard timing; either way, it could easily exceed 300 km/h with its 5.7-litre V12.

Unfortunately for both Jaguar and McLaren, they left it a little late. In the late 1980s, that time of wretched excess, there was enough *nouveau riche* money around to finance cars costing around half a million pounds or three-quarters of a million dollars, in realistic production runs. As it turned out, Jaguar had to sue a number of the people who had put £50,000 deposits on the £403,000 ($625,000) XJ220, and the real world price dropped by about a third, while

McLaren just never built as many F1s as they had hoped. That they built any at all was a miracle: this was the world's most expensive production car, at up to a million dollars a throw (the actual prices paid were not widely publicized).

The two approaches were very different. The Jaguar 220 had a race-bred twin-turbo V6 of just 3.5 litres delivering around 550 bhp (a lot depended on air temperature and relative humidity), while the McLaren F1 had a 6-litre V12 (designed by BMW) delivering more than 600 bhp: no racing pedigree in the engine, but with a McLaren chassis and that much power, who cares?

Porsche preferred an incremental approach, so they built on the basis of the 911. Admittedly, the 959 owed as much to the 935 racer as to the 911, but with a twin-turbo 408 bhp engine it topped 300 km/h with ease as early as 1988; indeed, at 315 km/h it was in sight of 200 mph. The 911 Turbo Coupé was closer to the road car, and could manage only 170 mph (275 km/h). Then, in 1995, the over-the-counter 911 GT2 promised 295 km/h, 183 mph, from a 430 bhp engine. Admittedly, it cost £131,000 at the time of its UK launch, $200,000, but with a Ferrari F50 at £330,000 (call it half a million bucks), that is not out of sight.

Porsche also hedged their bets in 1996 with the Boxster, yet another 911 derivative but smaller, lighter and cheaper: 2750 lb, 204 bhp from a 2.5-litre version of the flat six, and a top speed of 149 mph (240 km/h). That's over 250 lb lighter than the 911 Cabriolet, with 68 fewer bhp from an engine 1100cc smaller, but only five or six mph (10 km/h) slower, and about £30,000 ($50,000) cheaper...

There were numerous other sporting contenders, though many failed to live up to their initial promise. For example, a flat-8 which was to have been made on the Isle of Man was reported in 1993, but never seems to have amounted to anything; three Lamborghini-engined supercars were reputedly built by MiG, the fighter aircraft company; the projected BRM supercar remained elusive; and despite several impressive launch parties and even a handful of prototype EB 110 GT supercars (powered by a 60-valve, four-turbo V12 with 4-wheel drive and a claimed 212 mph, 342 km/h), the Bugatti remained semi-mythical.

On the other hand, Chrysler's 8-litre V10 Viper did make it into production with 450 bhp and a top speed of somewhere around the 300 km/h mark, even though the motor was originally designed for a truck. The TVR Cerbera had 350 bhp from a 4.2-litre V8, and about the same sort of top speed as the Viper. Lotus got 349 bhp from their 3.5-litre V8 in the Esprit, enough for a claimed 175 mph (282 km/h).

Drop your sights to 150 mph or 242 km/h, and all kinds of smaller fry come in, such as the Marcos (tested to 151.5 mph in open form by *Autocar* magazine in 1996: the fixed-head coupé was reputedly at least 10 mph faster). Similar performance was available from the Big Cat, Jaguar's XK-8, though that was closer in style and concept to the XJ-S than to the E-type and the XK120: it is a grand tourer rather than a sports car. Even so, 290 bhp from a 4-litre V8 and a weight of 3555 lb (coupé) or 3751 lb (convertible) give it 170 to 180 bhp/tonne and a top speed governed to 155 mph (250 km/h).

Once you go much below 150 mph, the rules start to change again. After all, there are plenty of quite ordinary-looking and indeed dull saloon cars which can top or at least touch 125 mph, so speed and even acceleration cease to be of paramount importance. What people look for is fun, which normally means light weight, an open top, and a spectrum of handling that ranges from the no compromise/no luggage school to the kind of car where you can pack enough for a long week-end. By the mid-1990s, the motoring press was wondering if too many such cars had not been introduced; where, they asked, would the buyers be found? We may yet be in for another Golden Age...

Right: the stunning McLaren F1

POST-WAR SPORTS CARS
1945–1955

No sooner was the war over than motor-sport started again: shakily at first, with most of the competitors (and manufacturers) fielding pre-war machinery, but also with an extraordinary flood of new designs, some of them worked out during long nights of sentry duty or as a relief from the realities of war.

Not just new cars and new designs, but new manufacturers were soon established. Ferrari, with their blood-red cars, were destined to become the greatest of them all, though the ageing maestro, Herr Professor Doktor Doktor Ferdinand Porsche, lived to see the cars that bore his name win races and establish another of the seemingly immortal marques. Jaguar cars — formerly SS, no longer a name they were eager to promote — revolutionized the sports car world with an affordable supercar: the XK 120.

Paradoxically, America was slower off the mark, though less devastated by war. Briggs Cunningham's noble attempt failed, in his opinion (probably correct) because he could not get the disc brakes he wanted. It was almost a decade before the Corvette started to capture the American imagination, still longer for the Thunderbird, while Ford's Mustang, in a sense a return to the Thunderbird's roots, would be delayed almost a generation.

Left: a 1953 Ferrari 375 America

The earliest Ferraris, like this 1950 166MM "Barchetta" by Touring, are (and always were) fabulously rare. To the modern eye, there is incredibly little under the hood – just a single carburetor on the V12 engine, for example – and while the body may be beautiful, there is not a spare ounce of weight on it. In the bare cockpit, there is no lining for the doors and there is no provision for weather protection. The Veglia "clocks" run counterclockwise; as on any racer, the tachometer is of course nearest the driver.

The 340 "Mexico" took its name from Ferrari's success in the 1951 Carrera Panamericana, one of the most grueling of road races, which ran right across Mexico. The huge flaring front wings are almost a parody of styling, and were aerodynamically far from efficient. Vignale bodied just three coupes in this style.

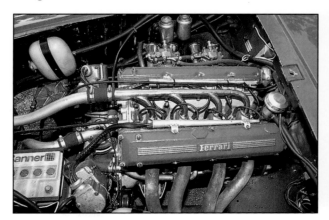

The 625TF is something of a mystery: a late 166-type chassis with Vignale bodies like the Mille Miglia cars, it was powered by a twin-plugged, twin-cam four-cylinder engine apparently identical to those used in Grand Prix cars. The "TF" name comes from "Targa Florio," for which the cars were apparently prepared; the vehicle is also known as a 625S. The first competition appearance of the 625TF was at Monza on June 28, 1953, driven by Mike Hawthorn. The car is liberally supplied with cooling scoops and extractors, but the overall effect is still a work of art, rather than being a mere mechanical contrivance.

The 375 America is a classic example of the way in which modern luxury Ferraris derived from the original light, Spartan racers. The 375MM (Mille Miglia), on which this car was based, was a no-compromise racer, but the same chassis made a gorgeous road car when clad in a body by "Pinin" Farina; this was before he ran his nickname and his given name together to become Pininfarina. The engine was downrated somewhat – by a little over ten percent – when compared with the racer.

The history of the 250 Europa is complex. The earliest Europas used the Lampredi engine, but the return to the Colombo design in three-liter guise marked a turning point in Ferrari's history. Only about 21 Lampredi Europas were built, but the Colombo Europa (later the 250GT) became Ferrari's first "production" car.

This Triumph TR2 is an early "long door" model: on later cars the door was shorter, and you could see the sill. More unusually still, it is fitted with a Shorrock supercharger, which probably gave it roughly equivalent performance to an unblown XK120. Many people regard the TR2 as the perfect 1950s blend of an old-fashioned "hairy chested" sports car with an unmistakable, unique look all of its own. The ride was distinctly bumpy and vintage, but it was a car which was quite easy to steer with the throttle. When it was built, it was relatively affordable at around $2500 in the United States.

The legendary XK 120, which appeared in 1948, was originally intended as a test bed for the new 3442 cc dohc XK engine. William Lyons is reputed to have designed its classic body shape in less than two weeks. The car used the chassis and suspension that had been developed for the proposed Mark VII saloon. Originally introduced as an open two-seater, the car was later to become available in both drophead and fixed-head coupé forms. The earlier versions of the car were fitted with aluminum bodies but in 1950 these were superseded by a pressed steel shell which, although outwardly identical, was radically different under the skin. Wire wheels became a popular option in 1951, the year that the fixed-head model *these pages* appeared. The fixed-head variant boasted the more luxurious interior appointments of the saloons; wider doors and a roofline that was fractionally higher than that of the roadster with its hood raised. Although all this led to an increase in weight, the FHC suffered little in terms of performance: it was still capable of 120 mph and had a 0-60 time of 9.9 seconds.

The new XK engine, on which the company was pinning its postwar hopes, was first fitted in the XK 120 sportscar of 1948. Encouraged by its performance and racing successes, Jaguar Cars developed a lightweight competition model – the C type – with victory at Le Mans as the ultimate objective. Three cars were entered in the 1951 race, which resulted in a convincing win for the C type of Whitehead and Walker. Shown *these pages* is a 1952 car from Ecurie Ecosse.

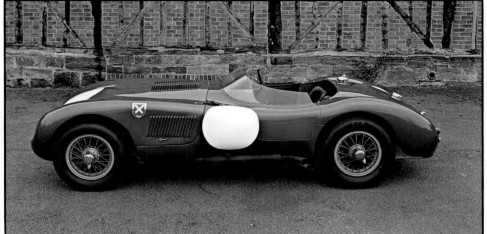

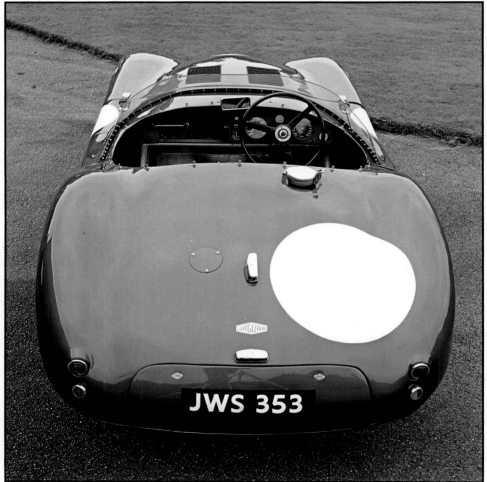

The XK 140, shown *these pages* in roadster form, was launched in 1954 as a replacement for the now ageing 120. The old body shape was retained but exterior trim was altered, notably the bumpers and radiator grille. The 190 bhp engine that had been a special on the 120 now became standard, and was repositioned to improve handling and increase interior space.

Power output from the D-type's engine was gradually increased over the years and fuel injection as well as various body and chassis modifications helped make the cars even faster. Shown *above* is the normally aspirated engine of a 1955 car. The bulge behind the driver's head *right* houses the fuel filler cap and on later cars this headfairing was extended into an integral fin that increased stability.

The T-series MGs were clearly a hold-over from an earlier age, though the late models like this TF from 1954 had incorporated a number of more modern styling cues such faired-in headlights and smaller wheels: 15-inch instead of 19-inch wheels had first appeared on the 1950 TD. The radiator cap was a dummy. On the other hand, construction was still very vintage indeed, with steel panels over a wooden frame.

By modern standards, power was modest: the final XPAG straight-four delivered 57.5 bhp at 5500 rpm from its 1250ccs, sufficient to propel the 1936 lb (880 kg) body at just over 80 mph. On the bright side, you could drive just about everywhere flat out: power, rather than handling, was what limited how fast you could safely go.

The MG was admittedly a good deal cheaper than the contemporary Triumph TR2 – about ten per cent – but the contemporary appreciation was very different from the popular view today. Instead of being viewed as a great continuation of a classic tradition, it was denounced as the outdated left-over of an old-fashioned line with inadequate performance.

Where it all began: a 1948 356/2, its Volkswagen ancestry very clear in the bulbous hubcaps, the tiny glass area (with a split screen), the spindly windshield wipers... Also, unlike its great contemporary the Ferrari (likewise launched in 1947/48), the body is practical rather than stylish.

The interior of the Gmund-built 356/2 seems somewhat claustrophobic today, with its high, small windows. The interior is Spartan, with modest instrumentation set in a plain, painted dash, and the cream plastic wheel does not look very sporty. There is also surprisingly little in the engine compartment.

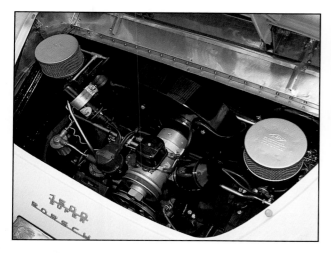

By 1952, when this 1500 Super America was made, the engine compartment was already beginning to look distinctly more crowded and purposeful, and the passenger compartment was very much more luxurious, with a much wider range of instruments and seats shaped to give better support. This car also has several period add-on goodies, including the hood straps, wheel trims and headlight stone guards.

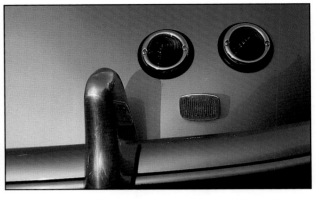

This 1954 356/1500 shows still more luxury on the inside, with winding windows, properly upholstered bucket seats, and "clocks" that go the right way – on the earliest models, the speedometer ran anti-clockwise. Also, this speedo reads to 120 mph (about 195 kph) – the original ran to only 150 kph. But the 4500 rpm "blood line," with 5000 rpm available for emergencies, still betrays the Volkswagen ancestry.

Each year, the Porsches improved. Not only does this 1955 356/1500 look much better balanced than the previous convertible, it also has better, easier-to-read instruments and a one-piece windshield for improved forward visibility.

To this day, the original Speedster is one of the most desirable and sought-after of all Porsches: this is a very early one. The lightweight, stripped-out body by Reutter of Stuttgart is beautifully set off here by the faired-in mirrors, the chromed stone guards over the recessed headlights, and the flat hubcaps with the Porsche insignia. The brilliant red paint helps, too! Weighing as little as 1650 lb, a Speedster is a reminder that power-to-weight ratios are about weight as well as power.

Colin Chapman's Lotuses – often referred to by aficionados as Loti – began as rather Spartan kit-cars. The original Austin Special first raced in 1948; the Mk 2, with a Ford 10 engine, appeared in 1949; the 1951 Mk 3 had an Austin Seven engine, and was the first to be offered for sale (all two of them!); the Mk 4 had a space-frame chassis; and Lotus Engineering was formed in 1952, selling the Mark 6 as a kit. This car, also known just as the Lotus 6, was generally fitted with either the 1497cc MG four or the 1098 ohc Coventry Climax engine. Some models – not the one illustrated – had motorcycle-type Amal carbs, which had to be "tickled" through blisters on the bonnet for cold starts in the morning.

When the new Corvette roadster came out in 1953, it was so radical that many people wondered if it would ever see series production. It was almost what today would be called a "Concept Car," with its stunning GRP bodywork and its handsome wrap-around windshield. It abounded in practical touches as well as in style; the stone screens on the lights may look a touch vintage, but they are a useful feature on a fast road car. The straight-six engine was a bit too vintage, though; more power was needed.

By 1955, the Corvette was a real production vehicle (though still not being made in very large numbers) and it had a real engine – a V8, advertised as "CheVrolet" with a curious mixture of brashness and reticence. The vintage-style stone guards still remained, and the three-speed gearbox was equally out of date for such a forward-looking car.

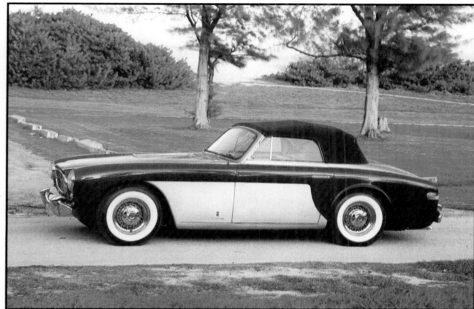

Losing $50,000 a year for five years pursuing a dream hurts even wealthy men like Briggs Cunningham. That's what it cost him in his attempt to win Le Mans with an all-American car. He came very close to achieving his aim with third place in his Chrysler hemi powered Cunningham C-5R. Much later, Cunningham was to say that if he had been supplied with the disc brakes he wanted, his car would have won at Le Mans. There's no reason to doubt his word; after all, in the 1953 race the C-5R was timed at 156 mph and the Cunninghams had the stamina to finish the gruelling 24-hour event while many

European racers failed. The car pictured here is not one of the racing Cunninghams but the 1953 C-3 "production" model. Styled by Michelotti, then working for Vignale, the Italian coachbuilders, the C-3 was one of only two 1953 American cars to be included in the New York Museum of Modern Art's list of the world's Ten Best Cars. Looking at the picture of the car taken on a late Fall evening in Florida, courtesy of the Elliot Museum at Stuart, it's not hard to see why it was picked. Under the hood is the powerful Chrysler hemi which turns this sleek grand tourer into a potent piece of transportation.

A radical design by Dutch Darrin was marketed by Kaiser as the Kaiser Darrin sportscar in 1954. Based on Kaiser's Henry J 100-inch wheelbase and powered by Willys' six-cylinder, 90-hp engine, the KD was a unique concept. It was built from fiberglass and came with sliding doors and landau top. Tail lights were lifted from the

Kaiser Manhattan and the odd grille looked like a pair of pouting lips. The car was quite versatile, with a top speed of 100 mph, and thrifty, with 30 mpg. The car shown on these pages is one of only 435 built before Kaiser went under.

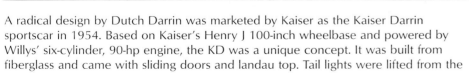

TURNING UP THE WICK
1956–1962

Old-fashioned sporting drivers have an endless series of euphemisms for going faster. They talk of turning up the wick, of pressing on the loud pedal, or of putting the pedal to the metal. Whatever you call it, the late 1950s and early 1960s gave them unparalleled opportunities for doing it. For most of the 1950s, Ike was president and America enjoyed an unprecedented boom — which they indulged by buying both domestic and imported cars, on a scale never before seen in the world. In effect, the 1950s lasted well into the early 1960s: the Swinging Sixties started several years after the decade itself. In Britain, Prime Minister Harold McMillan, also known as Supermac, told the electorate, "You've never had it so good." Indeed, by the end of the decade, they hadn't. From the rubble and bitterness of 1945, a new world had grown: not just in Britain, but also in Italy and even in Germany, divided though it was. The Wirtsschaftwunder had begun.

By now, Ferrari was the leader, by sheer dint of Il Commendatore's force of personality, but there was plenty of choice, whether your fancy turned to Italy, Germany, Britain or the United States. No matter what you chose, though, the general attitude could be summed up in one word: More. It was an age of power, only just beginning to be tempered by sophistication.

Left: a 1962 E-type Jaguar fixed head coupé

"America" was the name that Ferrari used for his larger-engined cars, and the word "Superamerica" was coined to describe his most luxurious car to date, the 410 Superamerica. Built with a clear eye to the American market from 1956 to 1959, this car (also seen overleaf) shows some American styling influences as well as an un-Ferrari-like regard for creature comforts.

The 250GT California was very much the brainchild of Luigi Chinetti, longtime Ferrari enthusiast and racer, and Ferrari's importer into the United States. The looks are a blend of American and Italian, but the performance is pure Ferrari.

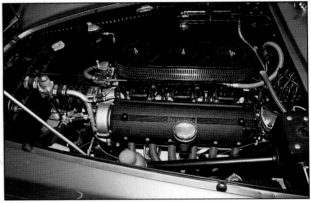

The first 250GT cars (also overleaf) were bodied by Boano/Ellena, and were surprisingly dignified and restrained. The front is reminiscent of Farina, and the rear of Michelotti, but the whole package was elegantly put together and made for the most practical Ferrari yet.

Launched in 1957, the XK 150's shape was noticeably different from its predecessor's: the waist-line was made higher, a curved one-piece screen was fitted and the radiator grille reverted to the style used on the 120. Disc brakes became standard and the new B type head improved performance in the mid-range.

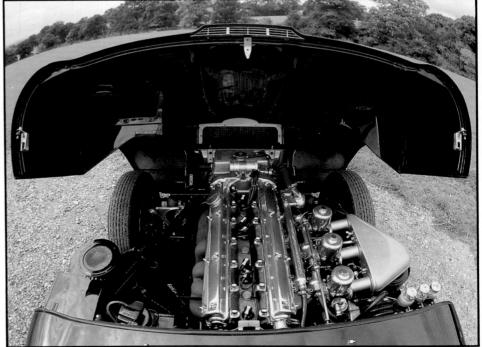

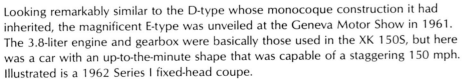
Looking remarkably similar to the D-type whose monocoque construction it had inherited, the magnificent E-type was unveiled at the Geneva Motor Show in 1961. The 3.8-liter engine and gearbox were basically those used in the XK 150S, but here was a car with an up-to-the-minute shape that was capable of a staggering 150 mph. Illustrated is a 1962 Series I fixed-head coupe.

The DB2 first appeared in May 1950. Like contemporary Ferraris, it was closer to a competition car than to a conventional road model. The DB2/4 was a 2+2 version of the DB2, introduced in 1953: it was followed by the DB2/4 Mk II in 1955 and the Mk III in 1957 (the "2/4" name was officially dropped, but most people continued to use it). This example is from the very last year of production, when it was known as the DB Mk IIIB. All the cars shared the dohc straight six, which grew from 2580cc and around 105 bhp SAE on the original DB2 (120+ bhp for the "Vantage" version) to 2922cc and 162 bhp SAE for the standard Mk IIIB – though the IIIB was also available with 180 bhp in uprated twin-carb form or with around 200 bhp with triple carbs.

The 356B of 1959 was the second restyle of the original 356. The much larger glass area made the previous generation look old-fashioned overnight, while the engines ranged from a base 60 bhp to a maximum of 130 bhp; this 1600 Super had 90 bhp, and a modest 5000 rpm blood line.

There may not be too much space for luggage under the nose, but who would complain? A proper, wood-rimmed steering wheel instead of a plastic ex-Volkswagen part, and styling which at last looked as if it was meant to be that way, instead of being a Volks that had shrunk in the wash – who would not want to see a 356B outside their door, beckoning?

In the interests of aerodynamics, the recessed headlights were covered with an outer glass shell, and increasing integration of details such as indicator and brake lights showed that the 356B had come a long way from a Volkswagen-derived "special."

Although better known for regal and indeed imperial limousines, Daimler always had a sporting side as well; there were some surprisingly quick sports-bodied Double Sixes before the war. The SP250 "Dart" was introduced in 1960 and manufactured substantially unchanged until 1964. The differences between the original version and the "B" and "C" spec models were that the later cars incorporated refinements which had previously been options: things like heaters and bumpers.

The SP250 was light (2090 lb, 950 kg), nimble and surprisingly quick. The lightness was due to the unexpected use of glass reinforced plastic for the body, while power came from an all-new hemi-head V8 engine of only 2548cc which delivered 140 bhp. In most conditions, it could top 120 mph with ease.

In 1957 the Corvette engine reached maturity: the immortal "Fuelie" V8 with fuel injection, and one bhp per cubic inch. The distinctive scoop in the side of the body had appeared the previous year, when the lights had lost their stone shield. A 140 mph speedo graced the dash, and well over 130 mph was genuinely attainable with the fuel-injected motor. Many regard the '57 *these pages and overleaf* as the ultimate 'Vette.

For 1958, purists bemoaned "the corrosive attentions of the 'stylists'," but by 1959 (when this car was built) some of the worst excesses had already been removed and the car merely looks exuberant today. Regardless of whether you thought the styling was better or worse, you had plenty of power. Even the base model 283 cid V8 delivered a useful 230 bhp, and the "fuelies" offered 250 bhp or 290 bhp.

Like all Corvettes, the basic design change of 1959 was refined for several years. This 1961 roadster (also shown on the previous page) is a 275 bhp "fuelie"; the front-end treatment and the "twin-scoop" cockpit are very much like the previous years' models, but the rear treatment is very different. The crease running backwards from the top of the rear wheel arch, and the flatter, less rounded treatment of the trunk area, may look very dated today, but at the time it was very much the fashion. If you look closely at the speedo, you can see that a 160 mph speed has replaced the earlier 140 mph model; and the fastest Corvettes really did need the extra numbers on the clock....

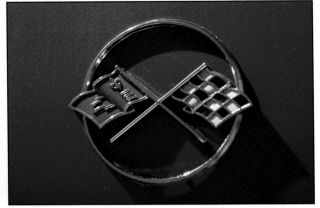

For 1962, the last year before the Sting Ray, there were not many changes to the bodywork – though it has to be admitted that bright red suits the design very well, and makes it look fresh and exciting even today. The 327 cid, 300 bhp motor that powers this roadster was only one up from the base 250 bhp model; for those who wanted more, there were options of 340 and 360 bhp.

Arguably the most attractive of the three-year cycle of two-seater Thunderbirds was the 1957 model, shown here. Slightly longer than the 1955/56 models, the last two-seat T-Bird had modest tailfins flanking the lengthened trunk area. A combined front bumper/grille treatment worked commendably well. Retained from 1956 was the optional bolt-on hardtop complete with glass "portholes" which was light enough for one-man operation. This fine specimen is on show at the A-C-D Museum, Auburn, Ind.

MID ENGINES AND MORE
1963–1973

At the beginning of the last chapter, I mentioned the Swinging Sixties. From the point of view of the sports car enthusiast, as much as from the point of view of the pop music lover, the dedicated follower of fashion, or the hippie, most of the 1960s and the early years of the 1970s had a lot going for them.

Prosperity was becoming the norm; people were getting used to it. Also, there was an overturning of established wisdoms: not always a good thing, but in sports car design as elsewhere a symptom of a re-think about everything. Instead of the old cry, "It was good enough for my grandfather, and good enough for my father, so it's good enough for me," people started to say, "But what would happen if...?"

As a result, the 1960s and early 1970s were perhaps an unequalled period in the history of the sports car. There were still plenty of hangovers from an earlier age of lighter, simpler cars, but there was also an increasing awareness that the whole was greater than the sum of the parts. Passion was augmented by science, and some of the greatest sports cars of all time were spawned: fast, yes, even by the standards of thirty years later, but also possessed of a character which many saw as lacking in later vehicles.

Left: a 1966 Ferrari Dino 206 SP

Great attention was paid to aerodynamics on the GTO (also shown overleaf). The rear "lip" spoiler and the low nose were both designed to increase down-force; the wind tunnel at the University of Pisa was used to refine the design, but the net result was still a car that was very beautiful, where art and science were combined more perfectly than ever before – and arguably, better than ever since. As befits a racer, a huge tachometer dominates the instrumentation.

"Superfast" was originally a Pininfarina styling exercise, a name applied to a series of four show cars built on just three 400 Superamerica chassis. When the Superfast 500 entered production as a successor to the 400 Superamerica, it was, however, fitted with an even bigger engine than the Superamerica, a five-liter hybrid derived principally from the Colombo design (with detachable heads) but with the bore spacing of the Lampredi block. About 25 Series 1 Superfasts were built from 1964 to 1966, and a dozen Series 2 cars followed. Superfasts were the most luxurious Ferraris obtainable, and they attracted a wide range of customers including the actor Peter Sellers as well as the Aga Khan, Prince Bernhard of the Netherlands, and the Shah of Iran – who bought both a Series 1 and a Series 2.

The original Dino 206 SP show car was a racer – and it showed. The mid-engined V6 was refined over several shows before actually entering production. It was a very forward-looking car, with alloy wheels instead of wires and a mid-mounted engine, yet paradoxically it represented a return to Ferrari's roots as a builder of small, light, sweet-handling cars based heavily on racing practice. Cars like the 500 Superfast had come a long way from those origins.

The production version of the Dino would have a somewhat less radical rear window treatment, though still with a strong reverse curve; the tail treatment would be less futuristic, and the ventilation slots in the rear would not be just black mesh. The engine would also be mounted transversely, and much less accessible.

By the 1960s, a racing car was so specialized that it could not really be used on the road: the day of the true sports/racer was passing fast. What Ferrari did, therefore, was to apply racing lessons to a car that was frankly too heavy and luxurious to be raced: a very fast roadster, rather than a racer. It was raced, and successfully, even at Le Mans; but the sheer weight of a 3600-lb. car meant that brake fade was always a problem.

The vast majority of the 1300 or so Daytonas were berlinettas (racing coupes), but a good number of "Daytona Spyders" were also built – about ten per cent of the total. Several berlinettas have since been converted into cabriolets.

About 4,000 iron-block 246GT Dinos were built, making them very much more common than the hundred or so alloy-block 206GT cars. The Targa-top GT Spyder shown here accounted for about 1,200 cars.

Now well over thirty years old, the E-type is still a stunning "good-looker" with performance to match. When it appeared, however, its impact can well be imagined. What amazed the *cognoscenti* even more than the pace from its 3.8-liter engine was its superb handling and road-holding, due in no small part to the completely new independent rear suspension. Here was a car that could be driven, even by the inexperienced, in considerable safety and comfort. Pictures show a 1965 Series I 4.2-liter E-type roadster, the larger engine having been introduced the previous year.

A new all-synchromesh gearbox, new seats, clutch and exhaust accompanied the arrival of the E-type's enlarged 4.2-liter engine. Acceleration times improved fractionally and increased torque coped with the unit's additional weight, but top speed remained at 150 mph.

Cosmetic changes, such as new bumpers and a radiator grille, distinguished the Series 3 E-type. More drastically, however, the track had been widened and wider tyres fitted, necessitating flared wheel arches front and rear. The roadster *these pages* now adopted the longer 2+2 wheelbase, and the 5.3-liter V12 engine ousted the straight-six as the standard power unit.

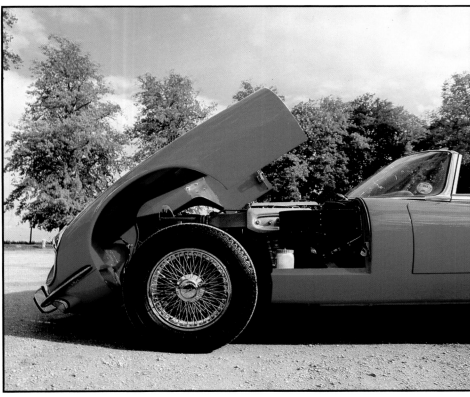

Shown *these pages* is the famous lightweight E-type that was raced by the German duo of Peter Lindner and Peter Nocker. Only 12 of these special, aluminum-bodied competition machines were ever built, and this one, with its modified Sayer tail section, boasted one of the most potent XK engines ever to have powered an E-type.

Increased demands on the E-type's 4.2-liter engine made by the American pollution laws, and the consequent downturn in performance, hastened the introduction of an all-new V12 engine. Capacity of the aluminum unit, which used a single overhead camshaft per bank of cylinders, was 5.3 liters. This exciting addition to the Jaguar range was unveiled in 1971 in the considerably altered Series 3 E-type. Illustrated is a 1975 V12-powered roadster, the air intake grille providing instant Series 3 identification.

The bigger "greenhouse" is much more obvious in this 1963 fixed-head 356B (also overleaf) than in the roadster shown on page 86. The "90" on the tail refers to the brake horsepower of the 1600 cc motor. Many people regard the 356B as the definitive 356 – the 356C is sometimes seen as a "stopgap" while waiting for the 911.

The very earliest Targas had zip-out rear windows as well as removable roof panels, but later models had a considerably more weatherproof fixed rear window. This 1973 2.4 liter 911T shows how little the 911 had changed since its introduction in 1964, though compared with a modern 911 the wheels are very narrow, there is hardly any flare on the wheel-arches, and the whole car looks severe and stark. The "T" engine, at 125 bhp, was the lowest-rated power unit when this car was made, and on the early "T" models steel wheels were standard instead of the now-trademark five-spoked Fuchs alloy wheels.

The 914 was Porsche's "ugly duckling" – this is a 1974 model. Mid-engined two-seaters are notoriously difficult to style, and Porsche made the mistake of assuming that they could get away with a brutally simple, functional look. Front/rear balance is superb, but unfortunate looks and disregard for driver comfort and convenience doomed the 914.

The front end of the new '63 Sting Ray was rather a matter of "love it or hate it." It was very much more modern (in the idiom of the time) than the previous generation, though the whole treatment had been foreshadowed by the rear-end treatment of the earlier cars. What really set the new Corvette apart from everything else, though, was that incredible split rear window. As a piece of styling it was without parallel, but for rear visibility, it left a certain amount to be desired.

The new instrument layout was much neater and more modern than the earlier models, though the instruments themselves were somewhat over-styled; the huge chrome centers and bent needles on the speedo and rev counter are more Detroit than Le Mans. The choice of engines ran from a 250 bhp baseline, through the 300 bhp 327 cid carburetor-equipped motor in this car, to a 360 bhp "fuelie."

"You can't beat cubes," is the way Americans say it. W.O. Bentley was even more forthright: "If you want more power, build a bigger engine." The 396 cid (6.5 liter) motor in this 1965 Sting Ray delivered 425 bhp, and disk brakes were all but essential to retard its progress. The one-piece rear window replaced the split screen after only one model year, making the split-screen Corvettes great collectors' cars.

Inside the cockpit, the dials had become much more purposeful – a recurring theme with Corvettes, where the stylists seem to get their way with each new model, and the engineers and drivers then refine the car each year thereafter. The '65 Sting Ray probably looks most beautiful in profile (right), though from other angles it still retained a magnificent brutishness reminiscent of the earliest Corvettes (overleaf).

This 1967 Sting Ray is powered by the awesome 427 cid (7 liter) motor, which could propel the car to 60 mph in under 5 seconds. Some cars had "sidewinder" style exhausts, which were illegal in some jurisdictions and which in any case were unnecessary. What could improve on these looks?

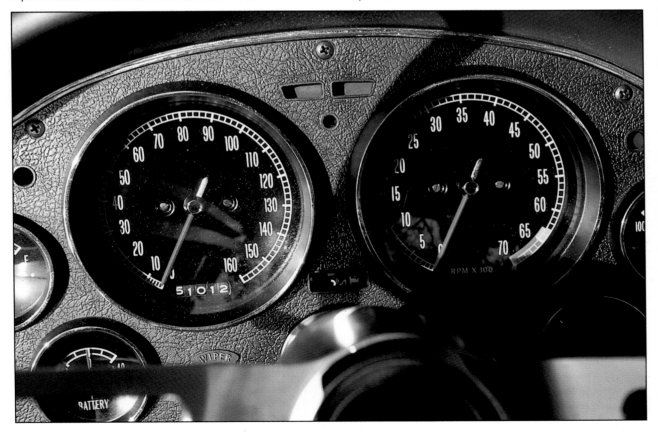

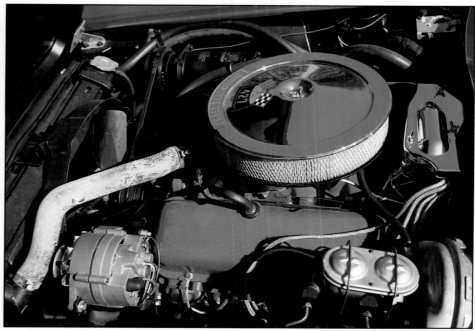

The Sting Ray coupé was such a *tour de force* that it somewhat eclipsed the convertible models, but they existed and, as can be seen from these pictures, they were very handsome. The lines are somewhat reminiscent of the Mercedes-Benz 190SL, but the American car has aged more gracefully; the 190SL was something of a parody of the 300SL, but the Sting Ray convertible was gloriously itself. This one is powered by the 427 cid engine; the interior already shows that happy blend of out-and-out sports and gran turismo which epitomizes Corvettes.

Once, many years ago, a Bentley raced the Blue Train; here the Blue Corvette faces no competition whatsoever.... The bloodline on the tachometer may only be at 6000, but the torque of the big 427 cid engine was in the locomotive class, and the solid chrome-ball four-on-the-floor transmits the power to the road most satisfyingly.

The Corvette as dragster. Taken together with the 427 cid engine and its 435 bhp output, the "sidewinder" exhausts have a certain inevitability. While this may not be the most sinuous or elegant of Corvettes, it has a sheer presence which cannot be denied, from the special wheels to the air intakes on the hood – and there are still thoughtful details like the spare wheel stowage (overleaf).

Each new Corvette, like this 1968 coupé with the 427 cid engine and no less than 435 bhp, is greeted with howls of agony and rage by those who reckon that the previous series Corvettes were the best ever. As it is steadily improves, it wins more and more devotees until even the die-hards confess themselves to be won over to the new style; then, just when everyone agrees they have got it right, they change it!

There is, however, no doubt that the '68 Corvettes were not fully "sorted" when they were released to the public, and there were even basic design flaws. The handsome-looking interior did not seem to be designed to hold actual people; the aerodynamics and cooling were wrong, and there were details such as the concealed wipers which simply did not work properly.

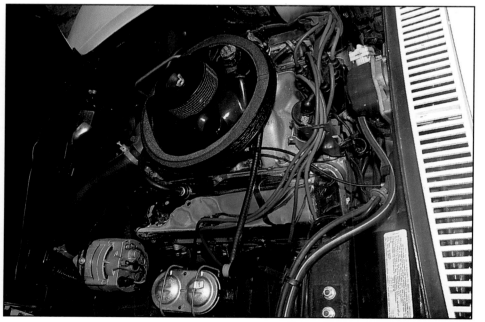

By 1973, the build quality of the fifth-generation Corvettes had been improved out of all recognition. The cockpit was slightly less cramped, too, as a result of a very expensive redesign. Despite the gigantic 454 cid engine, though, the power of this blue coupé is a remarkably modest 275 bhp – partly because the motor was redesigned to run on unleaded gas, and partly as a result of power outputs being quoted as SAE net instead of SAE gross.

In 1962 Carrol Shelby stuffed a 260 cid (4261cc) Ford engine into the ageing AC Ace chassis, and the Cobra (facing page) was born. It was later fitted with a variety of engines, up to the fire-breathing 427 cid (6997cc), and although it went out of production in the United States in 1968, it remained in (very limited, on again/off again) production in the UK for many years; in late 1996, a new owner was announced who promised to keep the Cobra alive still longer. This is a 1966 Cobra, from the same year the Miura (above) was introduced – the car which really put Lamborghini on the map, eclipsing the earlier 350GT and 400GT. The only major change to the Miura throughout its life was an increase from 320 bhp DIN to 355 bhp DIN. Power isn't everything, though: the Miura was tested at 160+ mph, while even the fastest Cobras rarely exceeded 140 mph. The Cobra was, however, a very dramatic car to drive, in more ways than one.

The new "Personal Car" from Ford was the logical successor to the early Thunderbirds – in fact, "T-Bird II" and "Thunderbird II" were considered as possible names before "Mustang" was chosen. With the V8 engine, the new baby Ford went as fast as it looked, too.

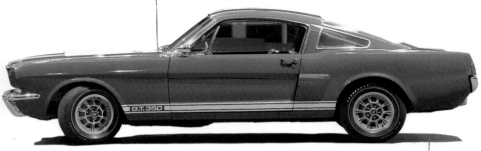

The Shelby GT350 was the first, and in the opinion of many the greatest, of the Shelby-modified cars that bore the Cobra name. It was most assuredly not a tractable road machine: in effect, it was a racer that had been more-or-less tamed and made street legal. It took skill to drive it to the limit, but unless you drove it to the limit, there was no point in having it. The early Cobras were not cars for poseurs: they were noisy, thirsty, uncompromising, and very, very quick. Even the late 1966 cars were not as blatantly racers as the 65s and early 66s; this is a 1966, and may or may not have the relocated suspension that characterized the ultimate Cobras.

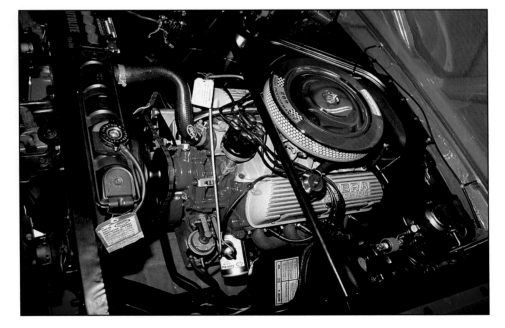

The 1967 GT500 was very powerful – the 428 cid V8, based on the Police Interceptor engine, delivered 355 bhp. A few cars were even fitted with the 425 bhp 427 cid engine. The big block motors meant, though, that the car was not as well balanced as the GT350, even if it was very fast in a straight line.

Rather than being an out-and-out racer like the original GT350, the 1967 GT500 was more of a flagship Mustang and a test-bed for new styling ideas – including non-functional rear scoops. The nose was extended three inches with GRP, while the rear deck lid was provided with a prominent spoiler. The GRP hood was unique to this model, and the scoop actually was functional. On most cars, the big driving lights were in the middle, as shown here, but for some states they were moved out beside the headlamps in order to meet construction and use regulations governing the placement of lights.

The Boss 302 appeared in 1969 and was powered by an up-rated version of the standard 302 cid engine delivering 290 bhp – 70 bhp more than standard. There were no fake scoops, the matte black hood reduced glare, and the rest of the matte black around the headlights and on the tail just helped it to look mean. It was one of the most functional-looking Mustangs since the original GT350, and the 302 cid engine meant that it was quite well-balanced and sweet-handling, so it was one of the nicest to drive as well. Fortunately for drivers, many people prefer the more powerful models, so Boss 302 prices can be (relatively) reasonable.

This 1969 429 Boss was powered by the 375 bhp NASCAR "homologation special" engine, and was extensively modified. A tendency to nose-heaviness meant that it required skillful driving at the limit, however; the 302 was an easier car to handle, but nothing like as fast.

The spoiler at the prow of the Mach 1 was not merely ornamental; with the 335 bhp engine, even the relatively unaerodynamic Mustang could be pushed along surprisingly rapidly. In place of the matte black hoods of yore, though, the hood was painted the same color as the rest of the body but with a central stripe which could be either matte black (as on this example) or white; shades of the old "up-and-over" Shelby stripe. Unlike some models, the 1970 Mustangs seemed to look as good in dark colors as in bright.

The "shaker" scoop that protruded through the hood, and shook with the engine, can clearly be seen above. This particular "styling cue" was borrowed from dragsters; it would have been equally possible, though less dramatic, to arrange for the ingress of cool air through the front grille or even via side vents. The engine itself owed most of its power to the old American saying, "You can't beat cubic inches," though more than 50 bhp/liter is not too bad for a big V8.

"All new for '70" was more than a slight exaggeration; the 1970 cars were mildly restyled compared with the major restyle of 1969. Even so, the cars were handsome enough, though replacing the outer headlights with imitation air-scoops looked suspiciously like a cost-cutting touch. The rear tail-light panel was arguably neater flat than it had been when it was concave, though the advantages of recessed tail lights are more disputable: they were quite hard to clean, and could be all but invisible when muddy.

The first generation of Mustangs – before the advent of the Mustang II – came to an end in 1973. The horsepower race was over (the most powerful engine available was the 266 bhp, 351 cid), and Ford had pretty much left the car alone for almost two years, pending the arrival of the new model.

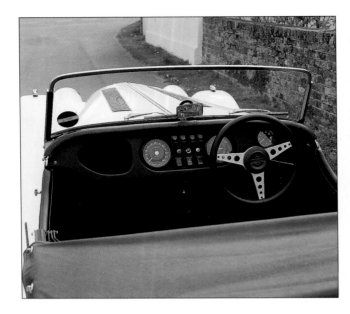

Morgans – "Moggies" – found their market niche and stuck to it. In 1935 they branched out from three wheelers, which they had been making since 1910, and the original 1935 4/4 is clearly recognizable as the ancestor of this 1972 model, and indeed of today's cars.

The biggest visual change since World War Two was the change from the old "flat rad" to the more modern curved radiator grille in 1954. Changes in power are another matter. The 1948 4/4 had 40 bhp from its 1267cc engine and could just about reach 70 mph; the 1951 Plus Four had 68 bhp from 2088cc and could top 80 mph with ease; and by the time this 4/4 was built in 1972, it had 88 bhp from 1599cc and could top 100 mph. Of course, if you wanted more power, there was always the Plus 8, with a V8 instead of a straight four. That gave you anything up to 184 DIN bhp in early unrestricted form, and 130 mph.

The ash-framed body is as traditional as they come, though some owners reckon the body needs at least one rebuild as the wood seasons. Purists, of course, maintain that modern Morgans have gone soft. If you drive over a penny on the roadway, you still feel the jolt, but you can no longer tell whether it is heads or tails.

The company has long resisted increasing production, despite waiting lists which have on occasion run into years, reputedly because they have yet to be convinced that sports cars are more than just a passing fad.

HEADS DOWN FOR THE FUEL CRISIS
1974–1983

As described in the Introduction, the fuel crisis alone was not enough to explain the long dry spell which characterized much of the 1970s and early 1980s. Rather, there was a failure of the will, a lack of belief in the future of the sports car.

That the causes of this automotive depression were illusory was demonstrated by those cars that did survive, including of course Ferrari. The Ferraris of the 1970s and early 1980s were not one whit inferior to those of earlier years, and there were plenty of others at the top as well: Lamborghini, Maserati, and at least for the first part of the period, Monteverdi and Iso. Nor could the Jaguar XJ-S be accused of being boring or bland. It may not have been another XK-120 or E-type, but it was still a pretty impressive motor car.

Rather than any real economic or technical cause, therefore, the problem seems to have been compounded of increasing fuel prices, the (prior) disintegration of the British motor industry (which had been so fertile a seed-bed for new ideas and designers), American pollution controls (which may have been justified) and safety regulations (which looked to Europeans like gross over-reaction), and perhaps an antipathy to the 1960s when everything had seemed possible.

Left: a 5.3-liter V12-powered Jaguar XJS of 1983

The strikingly handsome Berlinetta Boxer bore a family resemblance to the Dino but was clearly a much bigger, more powerful car, with the full complement of cylinders expected of a Ferrari: twelve.

The five-liter engine of the original Berlinetta Boxer was derived from the Grand Prix engine, and the 512BB was a larger version of the same thing. It is a very neat unit, but the extremely low lines of the car mean that accessibility remains a problem. Of course, given the kind of luxury that it had to propel, it needed to be a big engine! The engine-deck treatment, with the twin covers, would be greatly improved on the next flat-12, the Testarossa.

The XJS was introduced in 1975 as a direct replacement for the E-type which, it was felt, had reached the ultimate stage of refinement in Series 3 form. A hard top design was decided on because of legislation that, at the time, was expected to affect the American market. To minimize development costs, the mechanics of the new car were to be based on the already proven XJ saloon and the 5.3-liter V12 engine. The new car's shape met with a mixed reception and many enthusiasts, who had expected something as outwardly sporting as the E-type, refused to accept the addition to the family as a true Jaguar. With a shell design by Lyons and Sayer, performance equal to that of the E-type, and comfort and handling in the XJ saloon class, the XJS was, without doubt, in the best tradition of the marque. Shown *top left and right and facing page* is the standard XJS HE and *above left and right* a Lynx Engineering Spyder conversion.

Shown these pages is an independent but nonetheless stylish estate car modification based on the V12-powered XJS HE. Converted by Lynx Engineering and dubbed the Eventer, the car's advertising literature claimed a combination of "extra space, with amazing grace and thrilling pace." There can be little doubt that for the motorist who required estate car capacity and sports car performance, the Eventer offered the ultimate solution.

The MGA replaced the T-series in 1956 (first shown at the 1955 Motor Show), and the MGB replaced the MGA in 1962. Although both roadsters and coupes were planned, the coupe or MGB GT did not appear for another three years. It then proved extraordinarily durable: although it ceased production for a while, it actually returned with a variant on the Rover V8, and it was still available more than 30 years after its introduction. This has the rather nasty Mk IV bumpers, designed to meet American impact regulations: over 300,000 of the half million or so MGBs built from 1962 to 1980 were exported to the USA.

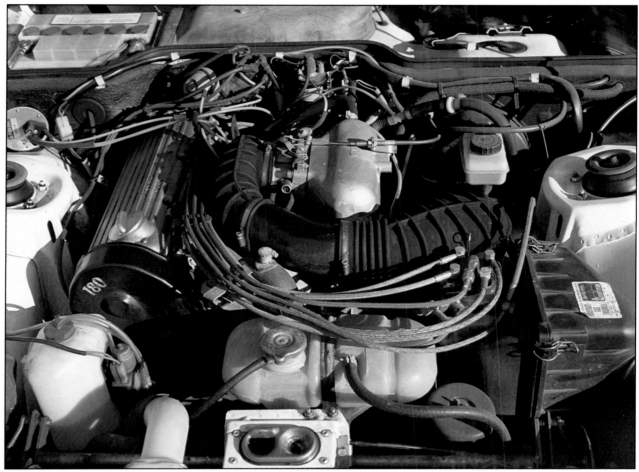

From any other manufacturer, the 924 might have been judged on its own merits, and seen as a fast, reliable, comfortable and surprisingly economical car. But Porsche is not just any manufacturer, and people expected more comfort, more smoothness, more performance and more individuality. As a result, the 924 is a surprisingly affordable car on the used market today. This one dates from 1977, a couple of years after the original introduction, and the year that the 5-speed gearbox replaced the 4-speed.

By many objective measures, the 924 is a better car than the 911: better front/rear balance, better visibility, more room inside. Its performance also compares favorably with the earlier 911 models. And against, say, a Toyota or a Lexus, it is more distinctively and originally styled. It lacks two things, though, when you stand it next to a 911. One is that "carved from the solid" feeling which characterizes the 911, and the other is an indefinable magic. The 924 is a very nice car. The 911 is, quite simply, a 911.

This 911SC dates from 1980, some sixteen years after the 911 first entered production. There had been many, many changes: more power, wider wheels, a more rounded body, shock-absorber bumpers...

Compared with that of the earliest 356/2 of 1948, the interior of this 911 – the seats, the trim, the instrumentation – is so much more comprehensive and luxurious. The trouble is that added luxury means added weight, so in order to keep the power-to-weight ratio reasonable, you still need more power.

The V8-engined 928 first appeared in 1977; this is a 1982 model, which bucked the usual trend by being lighter than the same model as originally introduced. By 1982, Europeans could buy the 300 bhp 928S, but Americans were restricted to the 231 bhp emission-controlled model.

The Khamsin was introduced at Turin in 1972 but entered production in 1974; the last one was made in 1982. It was a curious blend of the sporting and the luxurious, and it was the first front-engined Maserati to incorporate independent rear suspension. The 4930cc V8 delivered 320 bhp, driving through a choice of a ZF five-speed or a Borg-Warner 3-speed. At 3800 lb/1727 kg it was quite portly by supercar standards, thanks to power windows, power brakes, power steering (with Citroen hydraulics) and other gew-gaws, but it could do about 140 mph even in automatic guise and with the manual box it was good for better than 170 mph. The rear seat in theory made it a 2+2, but in reality, 2+1 or 2+luggage was nearer the mark. Production of all "classic" Maseratis was tiny, with 421 Khamsins made during its entire production life. This makes it rare even by Maserati standards, though the Kyalami is even rarer (150 examples 1977-1983), and production runs of several pre-1960 Maseratis were under 100.

By 1978, when this Silver Anniversary model appeared, the fifth-generation Corvette had been in production for a decade and was getting long in the tooth. Restyling was only skin-deep, but given the so-called "gas crisis," many people were grateful that the Corvette survived at all.

The long drop snout looked – and was – purposeful, but it would have been more effective with proper aerodynamics to avoid nose-lift at high speed. There is a sort of vestigial front spoiler beneath the air scoops, but it is not enough. Likewise, the rear spoiler looks suspiciously like a cosmetic afterthought, and while the big rear window increased interior space and improved visibility in traffic, it meant that the interior overheated rapidly in hot weather.

"Indy pace car" can be a dubious honor, after all, it's strictly reflected glory, and the car does not have to go particularly fast or handle particularly well. It's a good excuse for a fancy paint job and some dramatic graphics, though, and Chevrolet is to be commended for keeping the Corvette in the public eye in 1978, during a long period of dormancy when it could so easily have been forgotten.

The 1982 Collector Edition was the last of the fifth-generation of Corvettes, and was very much a Grand Tourer rather than a sports car in the traditional fire-eating mold. The big 350 cid (5.7 liter) engine delivered a miserable 200 bhp, and the car weighed rather over 3400 lb., so the power-to-weight ratio was a mere 128 bhp/ tonne; still very respectable, but a long way from the rocket ships of yore. Interior appointments, however, were very luxurious indeed, and the "double nickel" 55 mph speed limit meant that power was adequate for American conditions – at least for those who wanted to keep their licenses.

Perhaps surprisingly, access to the modest luggage area was still only via the passenger compartment, and the big racing-style central filler was a reminder of the past rather than a statement of intent. "Cross-fire injection" may have sounded impressive, but the sad truth was that emission controls, unleaded gas, and an increasingly outdated engine design meant that the specific power output was a truly appalling 35 bhp/liter.

cross-fire injection

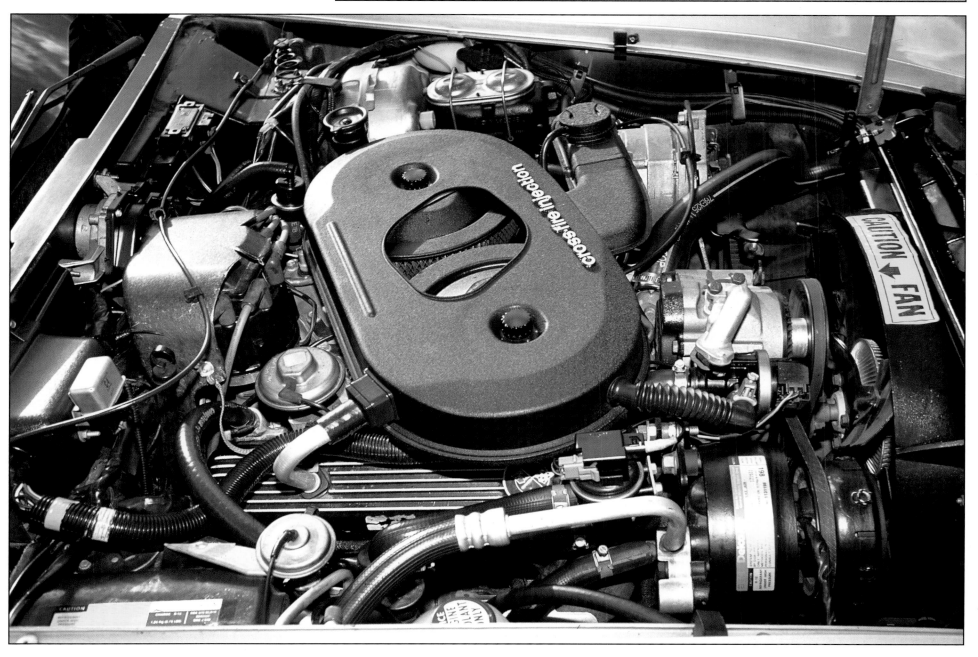

The right car in the right place at the right time: the dramatically downsized 1974 Mustang II met the demand, sparked by the "gas crisis," for economical cars. In the main picture, low-angle photography disguises just how much smaller the Mustang II was; it does however show quite clearly how the long hood/short deck styling cues of the previous generation were echoed in the new model. The rear treatment, with its integrated, multi-colored lights is very much more modern than the older tail-ends, while the area around the headlamps harks back to the previous generation's design and seems almost excessively styled; there are so many bends and curves in a small area of sheet metal that you immediately begin to fear moisture traps and rust. On the grille, though, the galloping pony unmistakably announces that this is a Mustang.

The 1978 model year saw the last of the Mustang II cars, which died largely unlamented. The $1277 King Cobra option was a cosmetic, wheels and suspension package for the top-of-the-line SportsRoof fastback equipped with the 302 cid engine (rated at a modest 134 bhp).

The styling of the King Cobra was love-it-or-hate-it. Those who loved it called it dramatic and original; those who hated it said it looked like a late 1960s record cover. Either way, both the paint and the brushed-metal dash look like period pieces today.

The 1979 Indy Pace Car Replica (also overleaf) looked much better than the 1978 King Cobra: the new body was a significantly better canvas on which to work.

Like the King Cobra, though, the Pace Car Replica was a cosmetic package, not a speed or handling package; the Old Faithful 302 cid engine now delivered 140 bhp.

RESURGENCE
1983 ONWARDS

The period from 1984 to the present may seem to embody so many contradictions as to defy consolidation into a single phase: from the wretched excess of the late 1980s to the recession and indeed near-depression of the early 1990s and the slow subsequent recovery.

At the top end of the market, that analysis is fair enough. In the late 1980s, and for the first year or two of the 1990s, it did indeed seem that there was a far bigger market for unbelievably expensive automobiles than turned out to be the case. Several manufacturers set out to build cars which cost US $250,000 or more, and at the height of the boom, such was the hysteria that the million-dollar automobile seemed a practical reality: some Ferrari F40s reputedly changed hands at this price, and the McLaren F1 had a list price around this level. In the event, many supercars were ordered by speculators who found their fingers badly burned, or by financial whizz-kids who suddenly found that sustaining very high incomes was a lot more difficult than attaining them. It seems likely (though far from certain) that the fastest production road cars which will ever be built, have already been built: the McLaren F1 and the Jaguar XJ220.

On the other hand, there was a certain amount of "trickle down," and less expensive cars multiplied apace. At slightly more than half a century after the beginning of our period in 1945/46, there were more sports cars around (by whatever definition you choose) than there had been for thirty years.

Left: a 1987 Porsche 911 Turbo Sport

231

The Testarossa was outrageous – but magnificent. Huge and immensely powerful, it boasted a 200 mph speedo and justified it with a top speed of 180-plus mph.

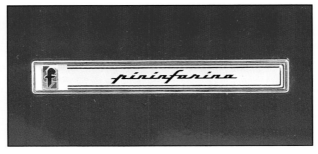

The widest roadgoing Ferrari built, the Testarossa was six inches wider than a BB and was exquisitely detailed. The engine deck treatment was a masterpiece of design, and underneath it lurked a 380 bhp version of the by now well established flat-12. It was definitely a return to the days when the mere sight of a Ferrari stopped people in their tracks.

To celebrate forty years of the marque, Ferrari built the F40: a stunning combination of good looks and sheer, unadulterated power. The massive composite wheels, thirteen inches wide at the back, were retained by hub-spline nuts and retaining clips; the body was made of ultra-light Kevlar and carbon-fiber reinforced plastic; and on the earlier models, there were absolutely no concessions to even basic luxuries such as the wind-up windows seen here. Originally, they were just sliding plastic. The distinctive triple exhaust (no mean trick from a V8!) comes from a massive collection/expansion chamber above and behind the engine, but most people would not even notice it – they would be mesmerized by the "wing" instead.

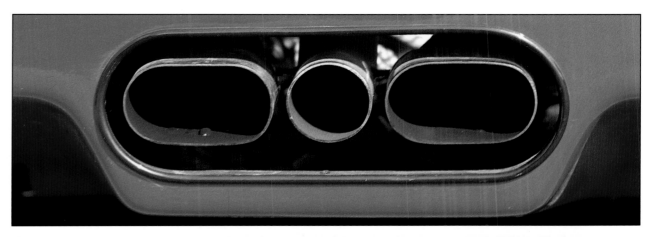

Which would you rather have: the car or the house? Lifting the entire rear of the car reveals the massive engine, and shows that the actual rear window separates the passengers from the engine compartment.

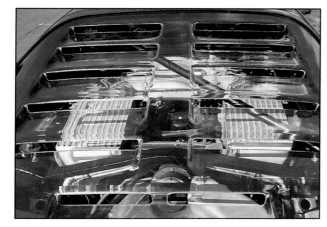

Facing page: a suitably regal setting for the magnificent XJ-S Coupé. Originally available only with the formidable 5.3-liter V12 engine (above) that served Jaguar so ably since its introduction on the E-type in 1971, the Coupé was also offered with the all-aluminum AJ6 3.6-liter engine developed for the XJS range. In its highly tuned state and bored out to a massive 7 liters, the V12 engine pushed the XJR-9 racers to a top speed of around 230 mph.

Whether in Cabriolet (facing page) or Coupé (above) form, there is no denying the beauty of the XJ-S. Long and low, the V12-powered models match the electrifying top speeds that were attainable in the fastest of the E-types, while offering the comfort and luxury expected of Jaguar saloons. With its accent on refinement, the XJ-S boasts a standard of handling that eclipses its rather more Spartan sporting forebear.

Unveiled at the Geneva International Motor Show in March of 1988, the XJ-S convertible boasts a power-operated hood, anti-lock braking, air conditioning and the super-smooth V12 engine.

The 911 ancestry of this 1984 935 is clear: still a 911 floor pan, albeit with a high-tech composite sandwich body, and such exotic trimmings as titanium coil springs. Despite having 590 bhp from a 2856 cc turbocharged flat-six engine, and despite really needing those brake cooling slots at the front, it still looks very much like a normal car inside – a far cry from, say, Ferrari's F40.

The 911 Turbo Sport of 1987 (also overleaf) clearly borrowed plenty of styling cues from the 935, especially the huge rear intakes and the dropped nose. Note the 6800 rpm blood line and the 180 mph speedo.

The glorious 959 was one of the wildest road-going Porsches of all time – a modern equivalent of the old 550, and much more practical than a 935. Clearly a derivative of the 911, it is nevertheless a far cry from its parent. Four-wheel drive with electronic traction control would have been impressive on its own, but a Kevlar-composite body to reduce weight, and no less than 400 bhp from a turbocharged engine feeding through a six-speed gearbox, made it very potent indeed. Top speed was certainly in excess of 186 mph, though a 200 mph speedometer, instead of 220 mph, might just have been adequate. To cap all this, it was also equipped to the point of luxury. The 959 was never officially "federalized" for sale in the United States.

The sixth-generation Corvette was first shown in 1982, but did not enter production until 1983 (the 1984 model year). To the uninitiated, it looked very similar to the older model, but it was an incomparably better car than its predecessor in almost every way: lighter, roomier, more comfortable, with a true "Targa" top instead of a T-top, and with vastly better access to the significantly larger luggage space. Improved aerodynamics meant that 140 mph was still in sight, even with the relatively modest 205 bhp motor; "Tuned Port Injection" was another of those marketing terms that did not actually translate into the power it promised.

The 35th Anniversary Corvette was a much better car than the 25th anniversary Silver Jubilee model, especially at high speed; proper aerodynamics kept the nose on the ground, and 245 bhp propelled the car at up to 150 mph on a good day, with zero-to-sixty times well under six seconds. The all-white seats were inclined to get grubby rather quickly, though they provided excellent support for driver and passenger alike and were very comfortable.

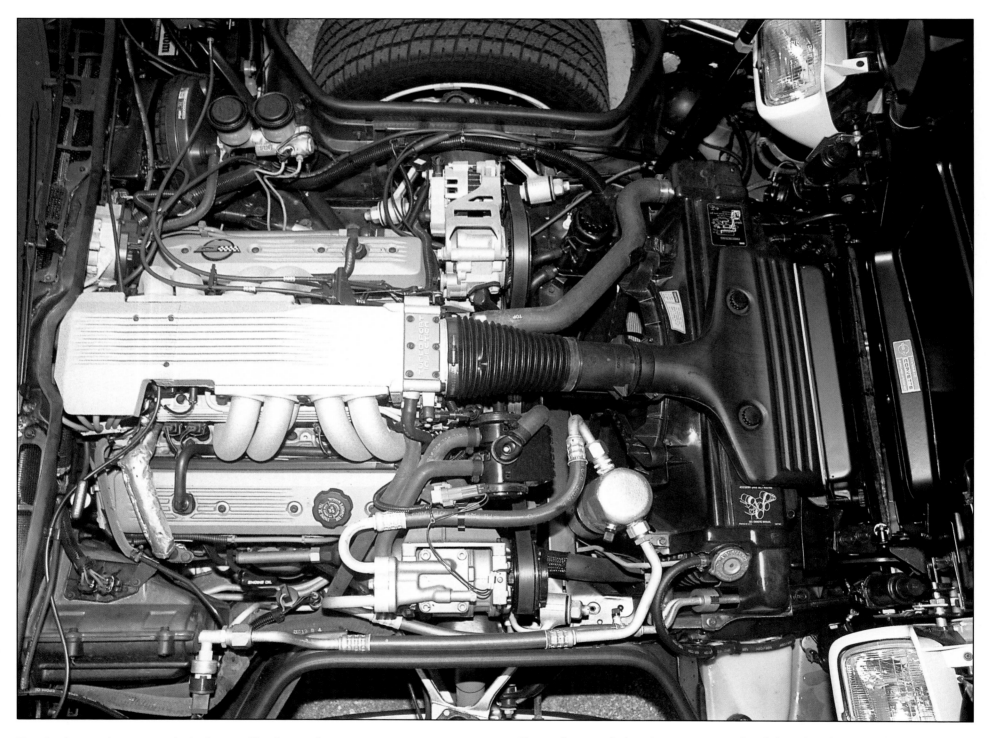

Despite the murderous complexity imposed by the need to meet emission regulations, engine access was excellent. The specific power output of the handsome white-finished motor was still not very impressive, though, at about 43 bhp/liter. For its first half-decade or so, the sixth-generation Corvette remained more a Grand Tourer than a truly ferocious sports car. The ability of its chassis and suspension to handle far more power than was actually available meant, however, that it was a remarkably docile car to drive, and only a foolish or inexperienced driver was likely to take the car outside its "performance envelope."

The stubby gear lever of this 1989 model controls no fewer than six speeds – a vast improvement on the overly-complex 4+3 gearbox of the early models, which was designed principally to finesse its way through EPA regulations. The power reaches the road through massive alloy wheels.

The Corvette authority Nicky Wright described the late 1980s models without the ZR-1 power plant as "a world-class sports car with an antique motor," and while this may be harsh, it is no exaggeration. The old Chevrolet V8 was never intended as an out-and-out performance motor, and although it gave a very creditable account of itself as the engine for a grand tourer, it looked very stale indeed next to its contemporaries. Though they might never require much more power themselves, the kind of people who bought Corvettes liked to know that a motor was available which allowed the Corvette to compete with Lamborghinis and Porsche Turbos.

At last, with the appearance of the LT-5 motor, the final piece of the jigsaw was slotted into place. Chevrolet were initially coy about the output of the Lotus-designed all-alloy V8, but it was generally accepted to be at least 100 bhp higher than for the previous version, with 380-400 bhp readily and reliably available if required in future. The six-speed gearbox now had plenty of power to transmit; the massive rear wheels could really get down to the task of laying serious power on the road, and anyone who was brave enough (and rich enough!) had a Corvette which could be steered with the accelerator pedal and the brakes, as well as in the conventional manner. Top speed was about 180 mph.

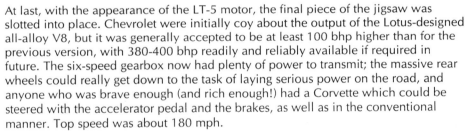

The 20th Anniversary Edition Mustang of 1984 (also seen overleaf) was a fine-looking car which sported GT350 side-stripes and 1965-type side emblems; but the majority were delivered with the 5.0 liter HO engine delivering 175 bhp – an improvement over the 134 bhp days, but still a long way from the peak power of the Muscle Cars. Others came with the 4-cylinder turbo. Interior appointments were much more luxurious than in the original GT350; but you would never have been able to hear a radio or a tape deck in a properly-driven Shelby GT350.

The SVO had the same 175 bhp power as the 302 cid/5 liter HO V8, but it achieved it in a completely different way: it was a turbocharged four of half the V8's capacity. The result was a relatively light, very nimble package which was however probably better suited to the European market than to American conditions: it was a car to be driven quickly and confidently on winding roads, but it was not at its best as a dragster.When fitted with the 5-liter engine it was its own biggest competitor: the V8 was much cheaper to buy, significantly easier to maintain, and considerably quicker from a standing start.

Despite its stunning looks and shattering performance, the XJ-220 was an unlucky car, which may yet go down in history as an also-ran. With a top speed of around 212 to 213 mph, it was for a brief time the fastest production car in the world – but then the McLaren F1 came along, even faster, even more glamorous, and even more expensive.

When it was originally conceived, the XJ-220 was widely expected to have a super-tuned version of the mighty V12 which had for so long powered other big cats, but it soon became clear that the weight penalty would be excessive, so they chose the same route that Ferrari had taken with the F40: a smaller, race-derived engine (albeit a V6 instead of a V8) running at impressive turbo boost pressures. Once again, from an engineering viewpoint, it was an entirely rational decision, and if the V12 had never been suggested, no-one would have minded. But from a marketing viewpoint, it rebounded on them: "real" supercars have V12 engines.

Then there was the name. Jaguar had cried wolf too often before, with the XK140 and XK150. When the XJ220 couldn't quite hit 220 mph, it somehow devalued the actual, very impressive speed of 212-213 mph in full emission-control trim and 217-218mph without the catalytic converters.

Finally, there was the recession. When the car was announced, it was oversubscribed. People paid huge deposits, without even knowing quite what the final price would be. As the recession began to bite, they melted away: Lloyd's names whose money ran out, and speculators who had never intended to buy the car, but merely to sell it on at a profit. Through no fault of its own, it became one of the worst symbols of wretched excess.

That's the logical viewpoint, anyway. But who could say, with their hand on their heart, that they wouldn't actually want one?

The F1 may well turn out to be the fastest series-production road-going car of all time, past, present and future, as well as the most expensive in inflation-adjusted terms. McLaren is of course a racing car constructor, but their intention seems to have been to build a remarkably practical and tractable road car – with blinding performance. Top speeds in excess of 220 mph have been reliably reported, and 230 mph does not seem to be out of sight. This is in a fully road-legal car able to meet American emission control requirements – and testers have also turned in 0-60 times of under 4 seconds. The statistics go on and on: 17-inch wheels, three seats (with the driver in the middle), 6-speed gearbox, McLaren Active Brake Cooling... The engine had no racing heritage whatsoever, but was a specially-built (by BMW) 6064cc V12 with four overhead cams and something over 500 bhp; indeed, on a cool day when the air is dense, maybe 600 bhp. With that much power and McLaren parentage, how much racing heritage did the engine need? The chassis is of composite Dyneema fiber, and kerb weight came out just over the magic tonne because they could not get carbon fiber brakes to work in a way which they considered acceptable for a road car. The car was first mooted in 1989, but the first "clinic" model was not revealed until 1992, and deliveries were scheduled to start late in 1993. The production run was smaller than was originally planned, because of the economic downturn of the early 1990s.

It was the Miura that established Lamborghini's name in the ultimate supercar league, with a combination of tremendous performance (even if power and speed were sometimes generously stated) and indisputably stunning looks. Thereafter, their record was patchy: cars tended either to be spectacular but impractical, or (reasonably) practical but not as exciting as they should have been. The spectacular-but-impractical thread reached its height with the Countach, but with the Diablo they managed to retain a good deal of the shock value of the Countach while building a car that was surprisingly practical and staggeringly fast, with a claimed 202 mph. Power, in traditional Lamborghini style, came from a big (5729cc) engine; and again in traditional Lamborghini style, the controls were seriously heavy.

The F40, of course, commemorated forty years of Ferrari. The F50, put bluntly, commemorates the fact that quite a lot of people then turned around and made cars which were faster than the F40. Inevitably, the F50 takes everything to excess. The 12-cylinder, 4.7-liter engine has five valves per cylinder: that's 60 valves. Like the McLaren F1, an obvious rival, the engine is normally aspirated: the F40, of course, used a much smaller turbocharged engine. But then, as W.O. Bentley so memorably said, "Supercharging is a perversion of design. If you want more power, build a bigger engine." Specific power output is 109 bhp/liter, in a carbon fiber body with magnesium gearbox castings and titanium wheels, and the whole lot weighs maybe 1230kg or just over 2700 lb (dry, not kerb weight). Top speed is a reputed 202 mph, though this might be more readily achievable with someone else's car than with one you had spent your own money on. It comes with a pair of tailor-made racing boots with the owner's initials, and two sizes of pedal box: one for up to shoe size 7, one for larger. But the proof of the pudding is, according to the old cliché, in the eating; and of the privileged few who have driven the F50, the general view is that it is a considerably better car in every way than the F40. Better appointed, easier to drive, more comfortable, but also better handling, faster on a circuit or on the road, fitted with a proper Ferrari V12 engine, and with even more of that indefinable quality which says – or sings – "FERRARI!"

The name emphasized the continuity with the old oil-cooled Boxer engines, but everything else was new: mid engine (not tried for a mass market Porsche since the ill-fated 914), water cooling, a new chassis, only 1250 kg weight (2750 lb), 48/52 front/rear balance (a 911 is around 37/63)... Also quite new was zero access to the engine from above: the only way to get to it is from underneath, on a hoist or (for the traditionalist) over a pit. This alone says quite a lot about the kind of reliability they expect. So, there are trunks (or boots, in English) both front and rear; and no hood (or bonnet) at all. Handling was the best of any Porsche, ever; the price was lower than the 911; and if absolute top speed is down as compared with even the tamer 911 versions, well, why do you buy a sports car? For handling; for fun; and for as much speed as most of us can ever use on the open road. The Boxster delivered all of these, in a car which was no longer idiosyncratic, and which offered arguably the finest compromise of its time when you take into account performance, reliability, practicality, handling and price.

A V10 engine is, according to some theorists, the perfect compromise between frequency of firing impulses, minimal reciprocating masses, and frictional losses. It is logical, therefore, that it should attract the attention of performance car designers. What is less logical is that anyone would make a V10, 8-liter truck engine; and what is scarcely believable is that someone would then put that engine into a sports car. Such, however, is the ancestry of the Dodge Viper. With an engine that size, a modest 56 bhp/liter is still enough for 450 bhp, with torque which defies belief. No-one seems quite sure how fast the Viper will go, because it is so noisy and brutal above about 120 or 130 mph, but 185 mph has been bandied about.

Weight is a surprisingly modest 3425 lb, and a 6-speed gearbox is a concession to sporting pretensions. The 0-60 time is around 4.5 seconds: only six-tenths of a second slower than the McLaren F1, at five or six times the price, but equally, half a second slower than the significantly cheaper TVR Cerbera.

After sixty years of straight sixes, and a quarter of a century of V-12s, Jaguar went to a V8. Regardless of why they did it, the engine was impressive: four cams, 32 valves, variable inlet timing, and 290 bhp at 6100 rpm. Then, to add to the novelty, they put it into a new car which weighed around 1600 kg (3500 lb) for the coupe and 1700 kg (3750 lb) for the convertible. Well, it was fairly new, though more than traces of the XJ-S floor pan can be seen if you look hard. Again, the reasons why they made the new body don't necessarily matter. What matters is whether they got it right, and the consensus is that they did. The new model went back to the old Jaguar watchwords of "Grace, Pace and Space," though it was only spacious if viewed as a 2+2 GT rather than as a true 4-seater. But the driver and front seat passenger were cosseted; there was plenty of real tree and real cow; and with a 155 mph top speed (1 mph less for the convertible) and a

0-to-60 mph time in the mid-six-second range, its performance was not in question.

Perhaps the most interesting thing, though, is just how international a car this quintessentially English Jaguar turned out to be. The gearbox was from ZF. Nippondenso furnished both the engine management electronics and the air conditioning. The sound system came from Alpine. Cylinder heads were cast by Cosworth. All through the design and manufacturing process, the sheer financial might of Ford allowed Jaguar to get the best components, at the best prices. And, of course, if Jaguar defined the early post-war years with the XK120, it could be said that better than 50 years on, they still had their fingers as much on the pulse of public demand as ever. You cannot cross the same river twice, and the XK8 is a very different car from the XK120. The really difficult question is which you would rather have...

With the number of BMW Z3 roadsters you see on the roads, this has truly been a winning number. The long front end and short rear are classic roadster features and the Z3 fits right in. Under the long curvaceous hood of the latest model, there lurks a 3-liter engine (taking over from the older 2.8-liter). This is an in line all new M54 version and offers considerable improvements in performance. It can sprint to 62mph (100kph) in 6 seconds and the front brake discs have been upgraded to accommodate the extra changes. The automatic gearbox has also taken a change and an extra gear has been

added, enhancing not only acceleration and top speed but also CO_2 emissions. Additional safety measures have been incorporated to give a better and safer ride in these conditions. BMW now offer the latest version of Dynamic Stability Control (DSCIII) as an option. In addition, Automatic Stability Control (ASC +T) ensures that the wheels will behave, even on slippery surfaces. Smart airbags make their debut in the new Z3 roadster. They can detect how bad an accident is and will only inflate to the required pressure to deal with that situation.

Back in March of 1989 when Nigel Mansell was still racing for Ferrari, he took his F1 car to victory in the Brazilian Grand Prix. Little did the general watching public know that it was fitted with their latest gadget, the electrohydraulic gearbox management system. He no longer had to fight with a gear lever, at finger length behind the steering wheel were two paddles that operated the up and down movement of the gears. Ferrari then went on to develop this system for the 355. Two versions of the car were produced, one was with the system and the other was the conventional gearbox version, designated F1. Today several models from the Fiat/Ferrai line-up are equipped with this system, which allows you to change gear in just 1.5 tenths of a second. The 355 F1 Berlinetta uses a Ferrari 90 degree V8 engine, it has a top speed of 183mph (292kph) and will rush you to 60mph (96kph) from standstill in 4.6 seconds.

At the Geneva Motor Show of 1999, Bentley presented a sports car study called the Hunaudieres. The name comes from the famous high speed straight at Le Mans where the Bentley legend was born in the 1920s with five victories in the "vingt quatre heures du Mans". This Bentley is like no other Bentley before it, using for the first time a mid-engine construction. The 16 cylinder engine is made up of two banks of eight cylinders which are fitted in a "W" shape. Both cylinder banks are made up of two rows of four cylinders. In this way the engine is also very compact with a length of 26 inches (643mm) and a width of 28 inches (690mm). The engine is made of aluminum alloy and has four overhead chain driven adjustable camshafts. A five-speed gearbox is used to transmit drive to a permanent four-wheel drive system, 20 inch tyres have been specially produced for the car. The interior is made up of Nubuck and Connolly leather in dark green and tan and engine turned aluminum, which mirrors some of the external parts of the car such as the spoilers, bumpers and entry areas.

Both the Coupe and the soft top Roadster Audi TT made their debuts, in concept format, in 1995. In June of 1999 a road going version of the coupe quattro concept was introduced in the UK. By 2000 the Roadster had joined its counterpart. The Audi TT Quattro Roadster uses a four-wheel permanent drive system and is only one of two open-top two seaters to do so, the other being the Lamborghini Diablo Roadster. The car is available in the UK in two versions, both using a turbocharged, 1.8-liter, four cylinder gas engine. The 225bhp version will sprint to 62mph (100kph) in 6.7 seconds compared to the 180bhp version's 7.9 seconds. Top speed of the cars is 147mph (235kph) and 138mph (220kph) respectively.

Both cars are fitted with a six-speed manual gearbox, and powered soft-top and an electrically adjustable glass wind deflector as standard. Safety fitments are driver and passenger front airbags, side airbags (head and thorax), ABS with EBD (Electronic Brake Force Distribution), EDL (Electronic Differential Lock) traction control governing the front wheels.

The TVR Cerbera began life in the early summer of 1993 as a styling exercise by TVR's team of designers, who were very quickly given the go-ahead to start building full-scale models. The Cerbera was unveiled at the 1993 London Motor show. Since then, almost every aspect of the car has been improved. Originally, the Cerbera was designed to be powered by the TVR Power Rover based engines but it was decided that TVR's own engine the Speed Eight, would be a more suitable power plant and it was the first roadgoing TVR to feature it. Although sharing styling cues with the Chimaera, the Cerbera is a completely new car with new brakes, chassis, suspension and a different construction method. It comes with three different engines. The Cerbera Speed Six, is fitted with TVR's own straight-six. The Cerbera 4.2 remains in production for those customers who prefer a V8 and the 4.5 gives a range topping 420bhp and 380ft.lbs. of torque. Getting to 60mph (96kph) in 3.9 seconds, 100mph (160kph) in 8.1 and 150mph (240kph) in 17.9, the Cerbera 4.5 is one of the fastest road cars in existence. With larger brakes, modified suspension and larger wheels and tyres, the Cerbera 4.5 offers the handling and braking to match its performance, stopping from 100mph (160kph) in only 3.8 seconds and also includes a Hydratrak speed sensitive differential as standard.

There is no mistaking this is a BMW, the kidney shaped wide grill with its two integrated spotlights is very distinctive. The powerplant is a high performance 5-liter V8 sports engine, with variable camshaft adjustment and an intake system with electronically controlled individual throttle butterflies. The nerve center of this unit is able to execute one million commands in just one second. The engine is positioned in a "front mid engine" configuration, giving the car a 50:50 weight balance between front and rear axle. Power is transmitted to the rear wheels via a reinforced six-speed gearbox and the car can reach 62.5mph (100kph) in just 4.7 seconds. A kilometer (5/8ths of a mile) can be covered in 23 seconds and a top restricted speed of 155mph (250kph) is obtained prior to an electronic control cutting off the power.

Lamborghini tell us that no compromise has been allowed with the Murcielago, it is the ultimate performance car. Tucked neatly away at the rear of the carbon fiber and steel body is the powerplant that can thrust this machine to over 200mph (330kph) and can cover 0 to 62mph (100kph) in just 3.8 seconds. The engine is an outstanding new 6192cc V12 producing 580bhp at 7,500rpm. Supporting this is a new six-speed gearbox, with forced gearbox lubrication.

Maserati's new Spyder is an impressive piece of machinery. When launched back in 2001 its high performance and desirability helped to outperform its main rivals. Ferrari now owns the company and the cars benefit from all the technology that that company has at its fingertips. When Ferrari took over Maserati, they closed down the old factory, cleared out all the old equipment, fitted new machinery and reinvented Maserati. The Spyder is fitted with an all-new, normally aspirated, light alloy V8 engine of 4244cc, is capable of a top speed of 175mph (280kph) and can accelerate to 60mph (96kph) in just 4.9 seconds. Helping to achieve these figures is the electronically actuated six-ratio transmission – "Cambiocorsa". This is a Ferrari F1 piece of technology and entails changing gear with two paddles fitted directly behind the steering wheel, there is no conventional clutch. Changing gear has never been easier or quicker. If this all sounds too high-tech, the Spyder GT version has a conventional manual gearbox.

Initially known as the concept model RX-Evolv, the Mazda RX-8, as it became, was shown at the Detroit Motor show in 2001. The car is powered by a normally aspirated 250bhp 1.3-liter rotary engine, coupled to a five-speed manual gearbox. This engine is positioned in a "front-midship" layout with the next-generation compact RENESIS rotary engine mounted 2.4 inches (60mm) further back and 1.6 inches (40mm) lower than the RX7.

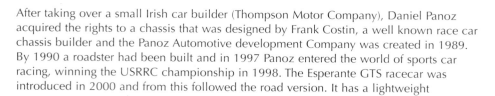

After taking over a small Irish car builder (Thompson Motor Company), Daniel Panoz acquired the rights to a chassis that was designed by Frank Costin, a well known race car chassis builder and the Panoz Automotive development Company was created in 1989. By 1990 a roadster had been built and in 1997 Panoz entered the world of sports car racing, winning the USRRC championship in 1998. The Esperante GTS racecar was introduced in 2000 and from this followed the road version. It has a lightweight aluminum chassis, which is bonded rather than welded together, making it an overall stronger unit. The body panels are produced using aerospace technology – SPF (Superplastic Forming). The power unit used is a Ford Cobra 4.6-liter V8, which is handbuilt by a two-man team and personally signed by them. This takes place in Romeo, Michigan at the Ford Special Vehicle Teams facility. Once fitted it can take you from standstill to 60mph (96kph) in less than 5 seconds.

Warren Mosler, owner of Mosler Automotive, has been building exotic sports cars since 1985, when they began developing and producing the Consulier GTP. It was in 1996 that Unigraphics designer Rod Trenne approached car builder Warren Mosler with the idea of creating a new American supercar, entirely in cyberspace. That car is the Mosler MT900, of which there are two versions, the MT900S for street use and the MT900R for racing. It is the first car of its type to have tooling machined from computer data rather than pulled off a handmade clay model. It is also the first supercar to be created entirely in cyberspace without the use of clay models or conceptual drawings of any kind. Trenne's data for the MT900 was so accurate that windshield and side-glass molds were constructed, from data, before the car was finished and fitted perfectly. The engine is an all aluminum overhead valve V8 configuration, it uses electronic sequential fuel injection and can put out 425bhp. Helping it reach its top speed is a six-speed manual gearbox. The street version comes with air conditioning, power windows and locks, ABS, traction control and a CD player. If that sounds too namby pamby, log onto the Mosler Automotive website and you can transform your mundane S model into an R model over the internet with a selection of extras that will keep any do-it-yourself guy busy.

In 2001 EVO magazine awarded the Pagani Zonda C12 "car of the year" status and the company has not looked back since. At the Geneva Motor Show of 2002 Horatio Pagani presented the latest Zonda sports car, now enhanced to C12 S status. This is an upgraded version of the C12, which has taken advantage of the continuing developments program that has been going on at the Pagani works in Modena, Italy

The car utilizes the huge 7.3-liter Mercedes-AMG V12 engine, replacing the 7-liter version, to propel it to top speed via a six-speed Pagani designed gearbox. At the same time to combat the problems encountered with the duo "enormous power" and "ballerina-like lightness", the company thought it wise to include a Pagani-developed traction control system. This should give the driver more confidence and the car better handling in all conditions. At the rear end of the car, the hood shape has been modified to give the driver better visibility. The rear wing has been split and moved backwards to give better downforce and improved stability at high speed. Inside the cockpit of the car there are all the usual suspects, air conditioning, power steering, hi-fi sound system, everything a driver would wish for. Leather (you can choose your own color and type) is used with extravagance and comfort has been made a priority. Although the rear end looks a little bulky and certainly different with its four exhaust pipes neatly positioned in a circular housing, the front is sleek and looks impressive with its twin slim headlights either side and its air intake positioned just off the road.

The company is Noble Moy Automotive. Lee Noble, the designer, who designed the Ultima, Ascari, Prosport 3000 and development chassis for the McLaren F1 supercar project. Tony Moy is the founder of the Page and Moy international motor racing travel company. The Noble M12 GTO can reach 60mph (96kph) in 3.9 seconds and 100mph (160kph) can be cleared in 9.4 seconds. The power unit is a Noble-developed, all alloy Ford Duratec V6 2.5-liter engine, mounted "mid transverse". Inside are four overhead cams, which work 4 valves per cylinder. Twin Garrett T25 water-cooled turbochargers help to speed up the breathing. A five-speed manual gearbox assists the driver in reaching these times and top speed.

Approach with caution, says the advertising for the Dodge Viper and you can understand why. The model has been around for a few years now and created quite a sensation when first launched. It could be classed as the classic American sports car with its aggressive looks and huge lightweight 8-liter V10 engine. With a top speed of 192mph (307kph) all transmitted via a six-speed manual gearbox with two overdrive gears, producing 450bhp at 5,200rpm it can hold its own against the best around, (the GTS-RT version is limited only to those with a competition license and is built strictly for racing). There are 18 inch wheels with high performance tyres to help you keep the beast on the road. Beware, this is a beefy motor, has good looks and should be treated with huge respect.